Joel Montague, Marie-Hélène Arnauld & Jim Mizerski

# CAMBODIA PAST
## Explaining the Present

A translation of
"Notice Sur Le Cambodge" (Notes on Cambodia), 1875

From the pen of
### Etienne Aymonier
(1844-1929)

Through the lens of
### Emile Gsell
(1838-1879)

DatAsia

2016

An Illustrated and Edited Translation of Etienne Aymonier's
*Notice Sur le Cambodge*, 1875


© Copyright Original Translation, Text and Design, 2016:
Joel Montague, Marie-Hélène Arnauld, and Jim Mizerski

Published by DatAsia
2016
www.DatASIA.us

ISBN: 9781934431627


Library of Congress Control Number: 2016949727


PHOTO SOURCE ABBREVIATIONS:
BnF: National Library of France
KMV: Kunsthistorisches Museum Vienna
MAE: French Ministry of Foreign Affairs Photo Archives

Front Cover Photo: A Musician at the Royal Palace, 1866-1879, BnF
Back Cover Photo South Gate of Angkor Thom, 1870-1875, MAE

# TABLE OF CONTENTS

| | |
|---|---|
| INTRODUCTION | v |
| ETIENNE AYMONIER | xi |
| EMILE GSELL | xiii |
| 1 - GENERAL ASPECT | 1 |
| 2 - LEGENDARY PAST | 11 |
| 3 - HISTORICAL PAST | 21 |
| 4 - THE CURRENT STATE - VARIOUS RACES | 27 |
| 5 - THE KING | 33 |
| 6 - DIGNITARIES - SAMRAP | 39 |
| 7 - MANDARINS OF THE INTERIOR | 43 |
| 8 - PUOK OR KROM | 47 |
| 9 - THE PROVINCES - EXTERIOR MANDARINS | 53 |
| 10 - PHNEAK NGEAR | 56 |
| 11 - CASTES | 59 |
| 12 - WATER OF THE OATH | 62 |
| 13 - REVENUES | 65 |
| 14 - TAX ON RICE | 67 |
| 15 - KAMLANG. - BUYING BACK OF DUTIES | 73 |
| 16 - RELIGION | 77 |
| 17 - SLAVERY | 81 |
| 18 - HABITS AND CUSTOMS | 85 |
| 19 - CELEBRATIONS AND FESTIVALS | 96 |
| APPENDIX | 107 |
| NOTES/QUOTES | 112 |

*"The past is never dead.
It's not even past."*

(*Requiem for a Nun*, William Faulkner, 1951)

Panorama of the western entrance to Angkor Wat, 1870-1875, MAE

# INTRODUCTION

Etienne Aymonier presented a succinct view of Cambodia in the mid-nineteenth century, as seen by an expatriate who actively observed and studied it for several years. It is a valuable informative record of that time and place. Knowing something of Cambodia's pre-colonial past, its culture, customs and traditions, is also useful in explaining Cambodia in the present.

In trying to understand present day Cambodia one might be misled by looking to western culture and traditions for parallels. Cambodia today came from a time when the kingdom was an absolute monarchy, privilege ruled over rights, justice had a price and freedom was at the discretion of the powerful. That was Aymonier's time; that was the past.

Aymonier's descriptions also inform us of the many admirable cultural customs and practices and the various annual festivals of that time, most of which have been preserved in one form or another. Any westerner who has attended a traditional Khmer wedding will recognize and appreciate Aymonier's description and explanation. His record of the annual festivals and celebrations document a culture that was vibrantly alive at that time, as it still is today.

Emile Gsell's photographs from the 1860's and 1870's are the best visual records of that time and place. The difficulty with which they were created should be recognized. In the mid-nineteenth century, photography was in its childhood and photographic film had not yet been invented. The predominant photographic technique was the "wet collodion" process. Each photograph required a glass plate negative to be coated with a soupy solution called a collodion, then dipped in a chemical bath that made it light sensitive in a darkroom or a dark tent in the field. Then the plate was placed in the camera back, the photograph captured, and the negative developed before the plate dried. Photographs could not be printed along with text since the "halftone" process had not yet been invented. So pictures had to be copied as engravings or printed individually and mounted on blank pages.

Finally, we want to acknowledge several institutions that made this current book possible. The online resources of the National Library of France, the photo archives of French Ministry of Foreign Affairs and the photo collections of the Kunsthistorisches Museum in Vienna were primary resources.

A glass photonegative by John Thomson, 1872, Wellcome Library, London

A nineteenth century photographer in the field

From *A History and Handbook of Photography*, Gaston Tissandier, Edited by J. Thomson, F.R.G.S., 1876

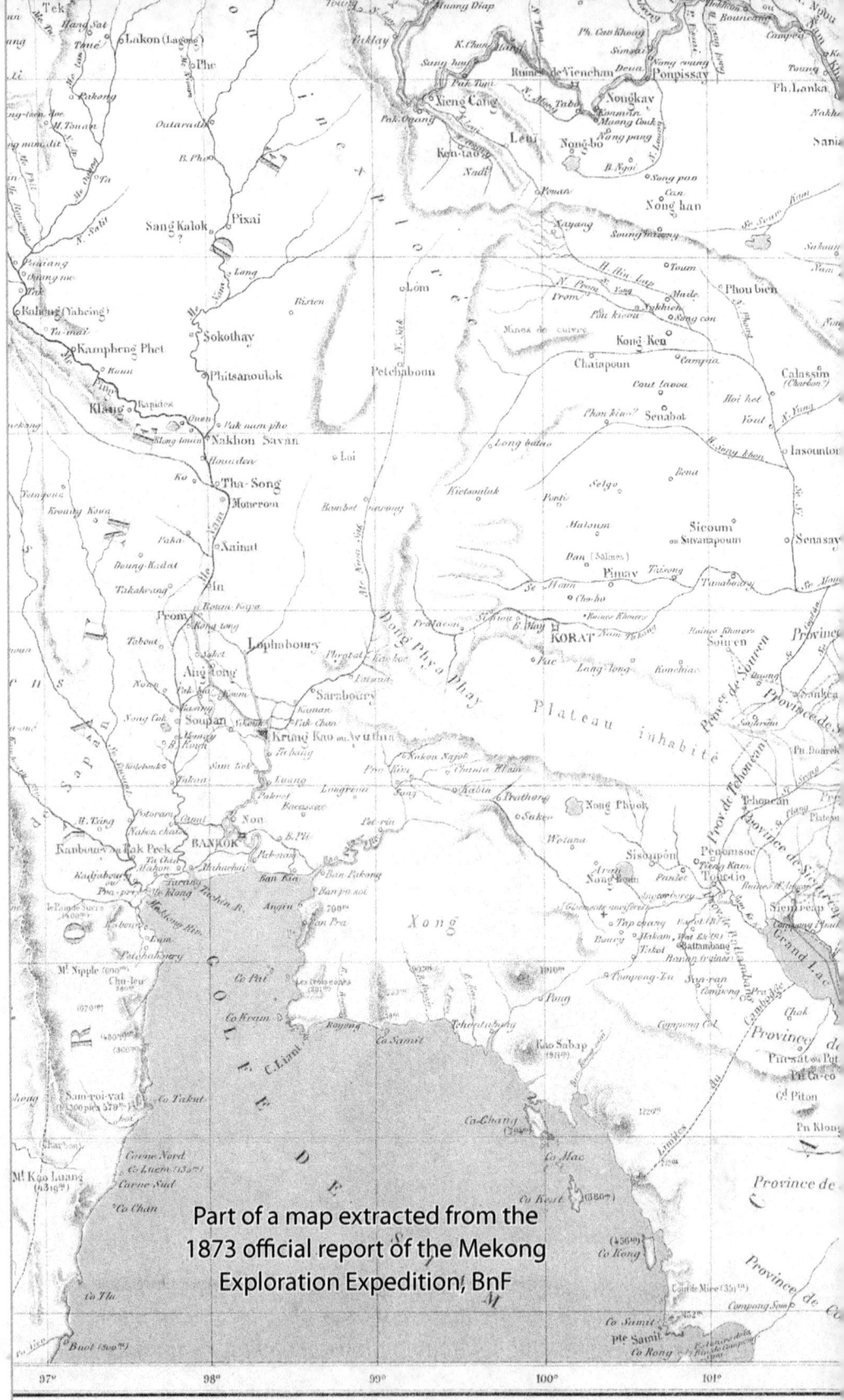

Part of a map extracted from the 1873 official report of the Mekong Exploration Expedition, BnF

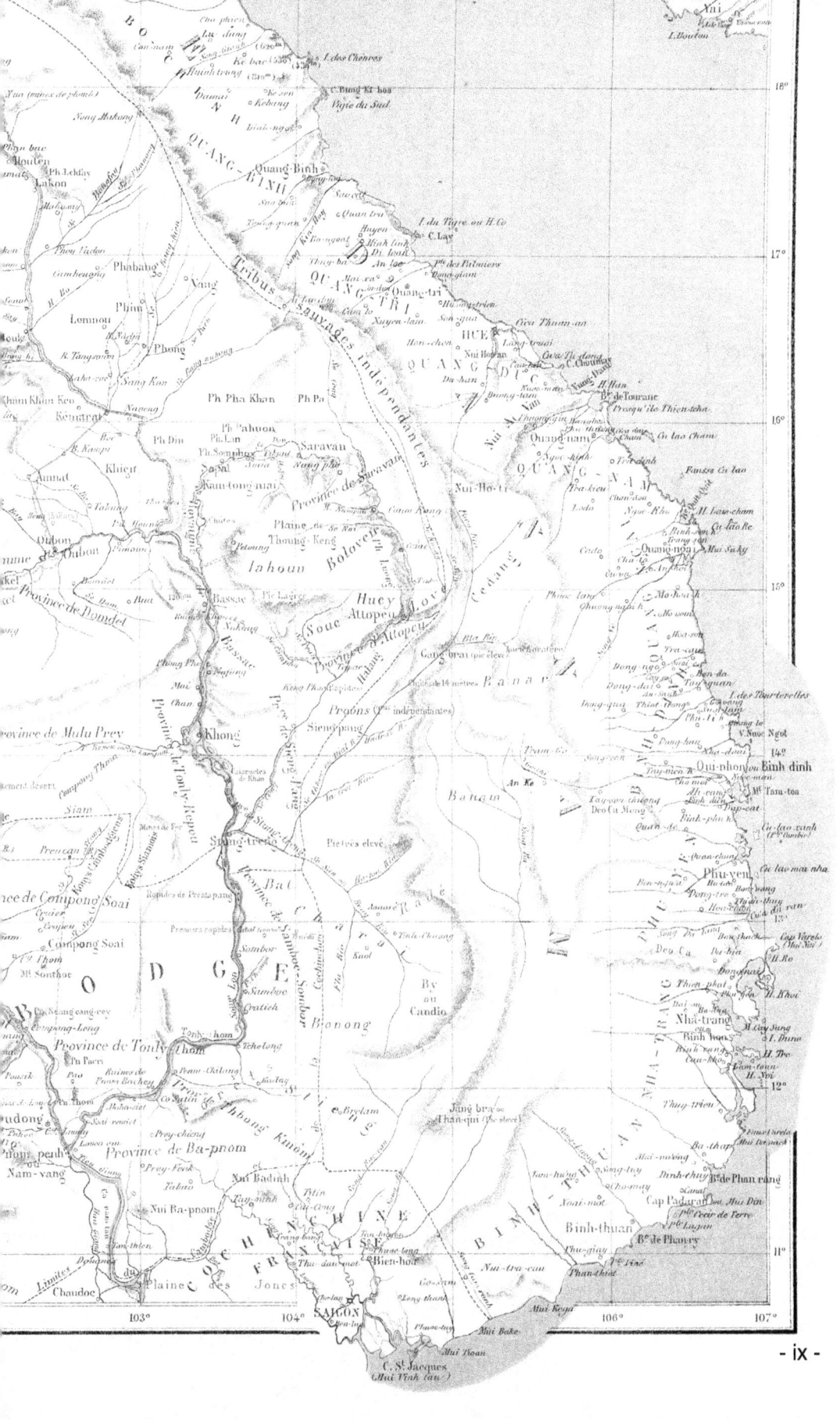

Etienne Francois Aymonier,
Photographie des Champs-Elysees, ca 1883, [BnF]

# ETIENNE AYMONIER

Etienne-François Aymonier was a French linguist, explorer, teacher and archeologist. He is credited with being the first to systematically survey and document the Khmer ruins in Cambodia, Thailand, Laos and southern Vietnam in his *Le Cambodge*, published in three volumes from 1900-1904.

Aymonier was born in Chatelard (Savoie, France) on January 2, 1844. At the age of 18 he enlisted in the infantry and in 1866 he joined the Saint-Cyr Military Academy and was appointed a second-lieutenant in 1868. Subsequently he was assigned to the occupation forces of Cochinchina and arrived in Saigon in October 1869. There he was assigned to the 29th Company of the 2nd Regiment of the Marine Infantry. In November 1870 he was appointed a trainee inspector of Indigenous Affairs in Saigon and in the following year he was sent to *Tra Vinh* in the Cham delta region of southern Cochinchina. At *Tra Vinh* he began his lifelong interest and passion for Cambodia, its people and its history and culture.

Aymonier advanced steadily in rank through the military administrative government and in 1873 he became the deputy of the Representative of France in the Protectorate of Cambodia, who at the time was Jean Moura. In 1873 he assisted Louis Delaporte with his Cambodian archeological expedition.

Promoted to the grade of lieutenant in 1874, with his being put in charge of the Government Department at *Hatien* he was tasked with verifying the delimitation of the Cambodian border with Vietnam. By that time he had acquired a knowledge of the Cambodian language resulting in him being put in charge of teaching Khmer at the college for trainees for the positions of senior civil-servants in Saigon. Also in 1874 he published his first two books: *Vocabulaire Cambodgien-Français (Cambodian-French Vocabulary)* and *Dictionnaire Français-Cambodgien (French-Cambodian Dictionary)*.

Etienne Aymonier continued to advance and on the eve of his return to France on holiday in April 1875 he was promoted to Administrator 1st Class. By then he had been responsible for the secretarial work of the Indigenous Department of Justice.

It was at this point in his career that Aymonier published the original French version of this book (*Notice Sur le Cambodge*) in 1875 and the following year he published another short book, *Geographie du le Cambodge*, considered a complement to *Notice Sur le Cambodge*.

In August 1876 he returned to Cochinchina and was again appointed deputy to the French Representative in the Protectorate of Cambodia. Then in 1878, he was appointed Director of the College for trainee senior civil-servants in Saigon and he published one of his most important books for learning modern Khmer: *Dictionnaire Khmer- Français (Khmer-French Dictionary)*.

In 1879, replacing Moura for two years, he acted as *ad interim* "Representative in Cambodia" (the French Government's highest post in the Protectorate). He was also promoted to the rank of Captain.

Etienne Aymonier's continued to explore, document and teach. The ancient Khmer archeological sites continued to be his passion and at the turn of the century he published his three-volume *Le Cambodge:* Vol. 1,.*Le Royaume Actuel*, 1900; Vol. 2, *Les Provinces Siamoises*, 1901; Vol. 3, *Le Groupe d' Angkor et l'Histoire*, 1904.

Etienne Aymonier died in Paris on January 21, 1929 at the age of 85.

# EMILE GSELL

Very little is known about this French photographer outside of his surviving photographs. No pictures of Emile Gsell himself have been made public, if they exist. Practically all published biographical information about Gsell, including this text, can be traced to the Gsell biography written by Jerome Ghesquiere in the book *Des Photographes en Indochine: Tonkin, Annam, Cochinchine, Cambodge et Laos au XIX Siecle.*

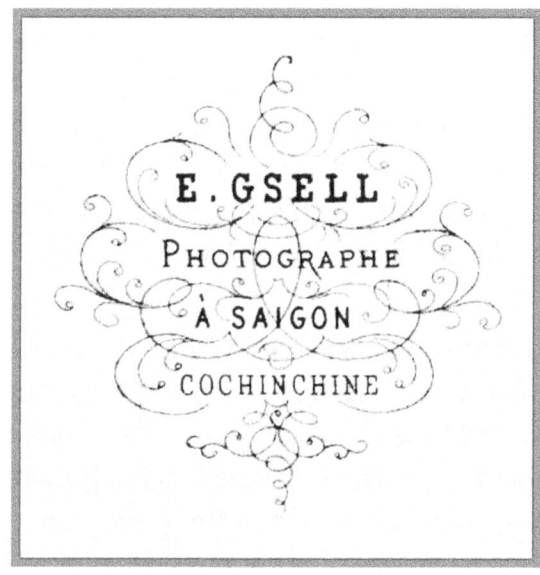

The back of a photo CDV by Emile Gsell, BnF

Emile Gsell was born on December 30, 1838 at Sainte-Marie-aux-Mines, in Haut-Rhin, an area that was ethnically German near the French-German border. His father was a canvas, or cloth, printer and he had a brother two years younger than he was. In the 1858 census his family lived in Paris and Emile was listed as having been called into military service. He may have been trained in photography in the military. Gsell was likely part of the French expeditionary forces of about 10,000 that went to China and Cochinchina. Since the normal period of military service was seven years, he was likely released from the military by 1865 and chose to stay in the East. An early record of Gsell's presence in Southeast Asia appears in Garnier's account of the start of the Mekong Exploration Expedition on June

5, 1866. He simply says that "a photographer from Saigon, Mr. Gsell, assisted the Commission during the same time." Emile Gsell the photographer appeared in the 1870's editions of the *Annuaire de la Cochinchine* (Directory of French Cochinchina) as a photographer at Rue Rigault-de-Genouilly in Saigon. In the 1879 directory he was still listed at the same address.

Although very little has been written about Emile Gsell, his career is nonetheless recorded in his photographs left behind in the collections of museums, government agencies, and private collections. He is one of the most important photographic figures, though still somewhat overlooked, from the early years of Cochinchina and of the early documentation of Cambodia, especially Angkor. His photographs have been used by numerous authors to illustrate their texts, sometimes without attribution.

Etienne Aymonier used many of Emile Gsell's photographs to illustrate his three-volume *Le Cambodge*, with proper attribution, although it was published over twenty years after Gsell's death. Fortunately by the time it was published, photographs could be reproduced along with text on the same page due to the invention of the halftone process. None of Gsell's photographs were included in Aymonier's original publication of this book, likely because it would have involved making engravings, which would have added significantly to the publishing cost. Nevertheless, It is likely that Aymonier was familiar with Gsell and his work in Saigon.

Ghesquiere records Emile Gsell's death as October 16, 1879, at the age of only 41.

Bas-relief at Angkor Wat, 1870-1875, MAE

# NOTICE

SUR LE

# CAMBODGE

PAR

E. AYMONIER

PROFESSEUR DE CAMBODGIEN AU COLLÉGE DES ADMINISTRATEURS STAGIAIRES,
A SAÏGON

PARIS
ERNEST LEROUX, ÉDITEUR
LIBRAIRE DE LA SOCIÉTÉ ASIATIQUE DE PARIS, DE L'ÉCOLE DES LANGUES ORIENTALES
VIVANTES, ET DES SOCIÉTÉS DE CALCUTTA, DE NEW-HAVEN
(ÉTATS-UNIS), DE SHANGHAI (CHINE)
28, RUE BONAPARTE, 28
—
1875

# 1 - GENERAL ASPECT

France, which seems set to recover the colonial empire in Indochina that she let escape in the last century on a neighboring island, took possession [by the French-Vietnamese war] fifteen years ago of the estuary of the largest river of Indochina. This river, called Mekong (mother of all rivers) by the Laotian people, Tonle Thom (Large River) by the Cambodians and Cambodia (name of the kingdom which occupied its mouth) by the first Europeans who came across it, has its presumed source in the very heart of Asia on the plateau of Tibet. The unexplored part of its basin [the land drained by the river and its tributaries], from the source to the northern borders of Laos, may be nothing but a long and narrow channel, considering the large number of mountain chains and water courses which diverge in all directions from Tibet.

The public attention at the beginning of the conquest [of Vietnam] largely focused on the middle basin of the Mekong, determined the audacious expedition of the [French Mekong Exploration] commission presided over by the dignified and late Commander de Lagrée. This explorer's conclusion was that one had to look elsewhere for the way to China.

Perhaps the difficulties inherent in a first attempt [to find a water route to inland China], the harsh suffering experienced by the travelers, had an influence on this conclusion. Perhaps also the imminent opening of the *Song Koy* [Red River] [as a route into China], whatever the results, will bring to the Mekong basin the importance that it deserves not only for the exploitation of its own richness, supposedly and rightly so and so important and varied, but also for the total security to be given to our position in Tonkin or even as a direct route of communication with China. It [the Red River] is certainly a less difficult and costly way than the one which the English with their persevering efforts are going to create from Burma to the Yunan province [in China].

In its already explored part, the river, around the 18° north latitude, veering off towards the east [forming today's border between Thailand and southern Laos], moves away from the western chain which continues to descend south towards the sea then curves southeast following the eastern coastline of the gulf of Siam, all the way to *Hatien* where conical summits scattered in all directions partly emerge from the alluvial plain and partly have their base still bathed by the ocean.

The eastern chain, squeezed between the river and the China Sea, sends numerous and short foothills eastward, shaping the coast of Annam into a narrow jagged shore which is indented by numerous gulfs, bays or natural harbors. This mountain

The lighthouse built by the French on the peak at Cape Saint-Jacques, 1866-1879. MAE

chain also descends towards the south and ends in *Binh Tuan* with its last peaks in *Baria* and in *Cape Saint-Jacques* looming up in the west.

A line, drawn from that last point to *Hatien*, would determine the entrance to a gulf which, in the early ages of the current geological era, penetrated northwest, occupying the biggest part of what today forms the lower basin of the Mekong, that is to say French Cochinchina and the Kingdom of Cambodia. This gulf was filled in by alluvion washed along by the river. This phenomenon was combined with that of the slow but constant uplift of all these regions. Today, the alluvion overflows and creates a point reaching out to sea in the form of the muddy peninsula of *Camau* (*Tuk Khamau*, black water).

The river, after having received the big tributaries of its enlarged basin, mainly on its right bank, rushes down from Laos into Cambodia, following the direction of the meridian line. Then it suddenly turns southwest as if to fall perpendicularly into the gulf it has filled in. But before it hits the western chain [of mountains] which runs along the gulf of Siam, it turns southeast following the thalweg of this big valley and flows into the sea through six large mouths.

Slightly below the bend from which it takes that final direction, first it splits into two main branches: the eastern or anterior river, and the western or posterior river. At the very point of this junction, in the middle of Cambodia, another arm, or rather another river, going up northwest and to which we will get back later, arrives and joins the river, producing the shape of an "X " This remarkable point is called the Four Arms by the French. The indigenous people give it a less picturesque name but with the same meaning: *Chado Muhk* (four ways).

It is under this name that the Portuguese knew the present capital of Cambodia, Phnom Penh, sitting in this wonderful commercial position.

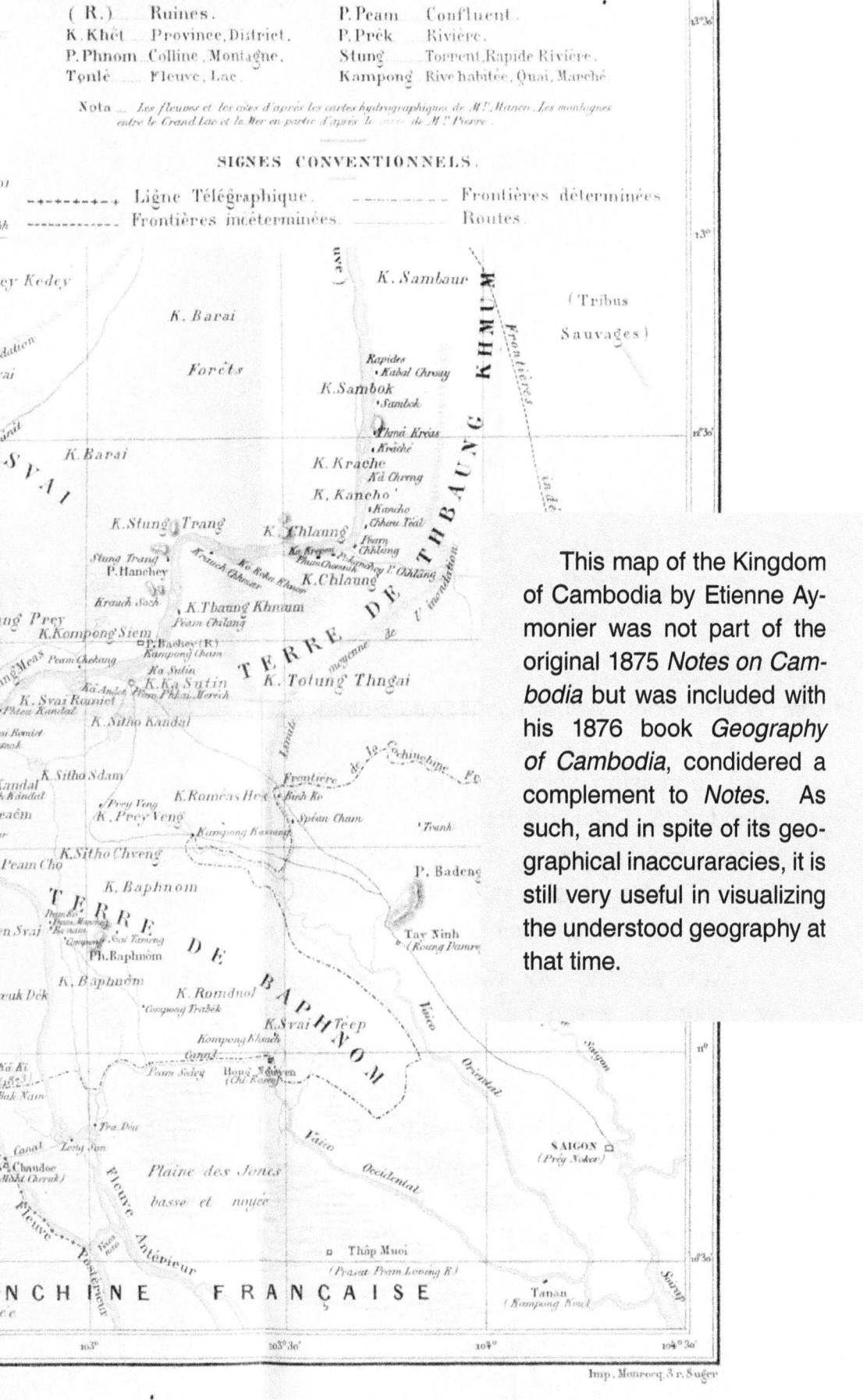

This map of the Kingdom of Cambodia by Etienne Aymonier was not part of the original 1875 *Notes on Cambodia* but was included with his 1876 book *Geography of Cambodia*, condidered a complement to *Notes*. As such, and in spite of its geographical inacuraracies, it is still very useful in visualizing the understood geography at that time.

Phnom Penh riverfront overlooking the Quadre-Bras (Four Arms), 1866-1870, MAE

An old bed of the river, or rather one of its arms, is indicated by a depression which goes down to *Banain* from the rich island of *Ka Sutin* and occupies the arc of a circle which at present the river makes curving to the west towards Phnom Penh. The Cambodian still give the name Tonle *Tauch* (small river) to the arroyo passing through this depression,.

Every year the river, swollen by diluvian rains, floods this whole region, which it seems to want to return to the empire of the water. Only the most elevated pieces of land form islands which are more and more rare and the area of which decreases depending on the strength of the inundation. The banks of the river, with a width of several hundred meters, are in general more elevated than the interior of the country and, therefore, the last to be flooded.

Numerous natural channels link the river with the plains via a double current, towards the interior when the water level is rising, from June to September, and towards the river when it goes down, from October to February.

From February to June most of these communication ways are dry and become roads, alternately being used either by carts or by junks. In the deeper ones, which are still navigable, there is generally a double daily current caused by the tide. At the end of the dry season, the tide can be slightly felt all the way to the Lake on the one side [the *Tonle Sap*] and to the rapids [of the Mekong] on the other. Once the flood has totally receded, lakes, swamps and ponds remain in the lowest parts and provide the inhabitants with water.

The far end of the old gulf, less directly exposed to the alluvial action of the river, has formed a much more considerable reservoir. In its length, it measures more than one hundred and twenty kilometres. It is the Lake which connects to the Mekong through a river [*Tonle Sap*] which also is more than a hundred and twenty kilometers long, and four or five hundred meters wide. It is through this perfect path, which completes the Four-Arms and heads back northwest from Phnom Penh, that the flood raises the water level of the reservoir [the Lake] by about ten metres, and covers in the far distance the low and swampy plains which are covered with grass, bush and mangrove surrounding the Lake and so doubles or triples its area, and as a consequence gives space and food in abundance to an incredible number of fish of all sorts.

When the water level is low, this aquatic population sees itself concentrated in the actual Lake, the depth of which has been reduced to one meter or even sixty centimeters. And so, from March to June, a remarkable industry of fishing begins. It is so abundant that, up till now, the nets, the salt and the junks seem insufficient for fishing, salting and transporting the fish. On top of the huge consumption in the kingdom, exportation reaches 7,600,000 kilos according to official figures, giving the crown an annual income of 208,000 francs, that is to say the tenth of the value given to Phnom Penh. This exportation is supplied almost entirely by the Lake. The product of fishing in the other lakes or in the rivers is consumed, for the most part, locally. The Lake and the river which links it to the Mekong is called, in Cambodian, *Tonle Sap* (fresh water river).

Flooding takes place, with all its strength, only in Cambodia. Further south in Cochinchina, weakened by numerous natural irrigations and finding several wide mouths into the ocean, it gradually loses its intensity and in the end gives the ebb tide a considerable superiority over the flow. Sailing up the river when the water is low, one can see the banks progressively rising from *Sadec*, where they are hardly above the level of the high tides, all the way to the rapids where the river runs between two twelve meter steep banks. This progressive increase in height along the whole way indicates the unevenness of the flood which fills the riverbed to the edges.

The mountainous region in the south, still little known, seems to detach a powerful branch which narrows the Lake near *Pursat*, and an extension of which, in the east, crosses the *Tonle Sap* river at *Kompong Chhnang* and closes the throat of the Lake, at which it separates the basin from the *Tonle Sap* river. The later stretches northward through the arroyos of *Stung Chinit* and *Muk Kompul* which allow it, for the first one, to inundate the provinces of *Kompong Soai* partially, of *Barai* and of *Prey Kedey*; for the second one, to inundate the provinces of *Muk Kompul, Kang Meas, Choeùng Prey* and *Kompong Siem*. Another branch of the southern chain, detached from *Kampot*, goes and expands to the north and to the south of the channel of *Chaudoc* at *Hatien*.

The basin of the Lake and that of the *Tonle Sap* river are separated from Laos and from the *Tonle Repou River*, that is to say from the middle basin of the Mekong, by a chain of hills, or a rather high plateau which stretches from west to east more or less following a line which is parallel to the equator.

Almost all these mountains, and mainly those of *Pursat*, are remarkably suited to the exploitation and cultivation of vanilla, gamboge and cardamom.

Phnom Penh looking north, 1870-1873, MAE

Ruins at the Bayone in Angkor Thom, 1871-1875, MAE

# 2 - LEGENDARY PAST

In the formation of this land, called since the remotest times, Land of the *Thelok* (*Kouk Thelok*) from the name of a very common tree, the fruit of which is very nutritious, Cambodian people have built their houses on stilts on the banks of the river, near the Lake or in forests rich in delicious fruit. (The forest north of Angkor has that kind of reputation). They also settled in the mountainous region which stretches in the south between the river and the sea,

A Cambodian village along the river, 1866-1875, MAE

a region apparently and especially called *Kampouchea*, a word which can be broken down into three parts, indicating a race: the tribe of *Kam*. One trace of this appellation remains in *Kampot*, Cambodia's present port. The tribe of *Kam* was perhaps one of the primitive tribes having lived in that country for a long time. Prosperous enough, it may have expanded a lot by absorbing the Hindu civilisation long before the introduction of Buddhism, and its primitive state could partially be studied today in its less known brothers, the *Kouys* and the *Samre*, still living on the high grounds north and south of the Lake. As for the name Khmer, it may have been introduced by the civilizers and, according to the most competent Cambodians (if there are any), the expression Khmer d'om (Khmer from the origin) may not refer to any particular semi-wild tribe nowadays, but to the unknown and remote people from which these civilizers came.

Their initiation to this ancient civilization gave the people of *Kampouchea* an unprecedented expansion, a great artistic development which can be attested by the magnificent ruins which cover the Khmer land, and by the vague traditions about the main characters of this unknown epic: *Bautumo Saurivong* (Lotus, son of the sun), the founder of Angkor; *Sangka Chahk* (the Discus of the Assembly); *Prea ket Mealea* (the Divine Glow of Gold); Indra's favourite (*Prea En*), to whom tradition attributes the construction of Angkor Wat; *Sdach Komlong* (the leprous king).

The appearance of a religion with pure morality thus found the people constituted Khmer, who had their main center near the Lake. It was the town of Indra, *Enthipat borey* (*Indra prastha poura*), which was later called Angkor or *Nokor* (the Royal town?). The enthusiasm, typical of a neophyte, of this people made them cover their sandy plains with pious works, religious buildings, dig artificial lakes (*sra*) everywhere to provide everyone with water and cultivate the sacred water lily.

Here is how a tradition describes the introduction of Buddhism: In the country of the sanskrit there was a very talented and knowledgable Brahman who, having embraced Buddha's religion, was soon familiar with the texts of the 'Three Baskets' (*Prea Trey Bey Dak*) containing the teaching (*Prea Saub*), the discipline (*Prea Viney*) and the metaphysics (*Prea Apithom*). But in the kingdom of the sanskrit, complete copies were rare. Realizing this, the Brahman ordered a *phikou* (*bhikhsous*, a beggar) named *Khosa*, to travel to Ceylon (*Langka Singhala*) in order to completely transcribe the divine texts so that, in the country of the sanskrit, all the believers were able to study them. The *phikou Khosa* obeyed, and this gigantic work quickly achieved thanks to the wonderful power of his stylet [a writing implement], he went and bid farewell to the head of the monks and to the king of Ceylon.

The king, being aware of *phikou Khosa*'s great reputation, invited him to *preach*. *Phikou Khosa* spoke with so much eloquence and persuasion that his audience compared him with Buddha during the time when, still on this earth, the Master was teaching the Law to angels and people. The king, who was enchanted, called him Buddha *Khosa* (*Preat Put Khosa*), raising him in this way above all human beings. The entire population of Ceylon ratified this glorious title through acclamation.

Buddha *Khosa* having had his boat prepared and the texts of the Three Baskets carried on board chose a favorable day to leave Ceylon and sail to the country of the sanskrit.

At that time, the divine Indra, king of the angels (*Prea Entrea Thireech*), thought: "In the kingdom of *Enthipat Borey, Prea Ket Mealea* is reigning. This prince is wise and his subjects are happy. But they ignore the religion of Buddha which guides people onto the right track, and *Khosa* is sailing towards the country of the sanskrit where this doctrine is well known." Then Indra ordered the Angel of the Wind (*Prea Peey*) to blow so *Khosa*'s boat would sail towards the coasts of *Enthipat Borey*. The boat, pushed by a strong wind, lost its route and ended up at the port of Kampot where, all of a sudden, the wind stopped. *Prea Ket Mealea*, informed of this by the mandarins in Kampot, full of joy came out of the towers of Angkor which he used as his palace.

Accompanied by his whole court, he sailed to *Kampot*, bowed at the feet of Buddha *Khosa*, begging him to come and teach him and his people the New Law. Back in Angkor, in the company of the holy man, he changed the purpose of the towers. After having richly adorned the interior, he offered them to Buddha *Khosa* who converted them into a pagoda for his teaching. From that day, in the whole of the kingdom, there was a big surge to study the Good Law which, from there, spread into Laos and Siam.

If this tradition was worth believing in, it would provide a precious date for the introduction of Buddhism and for *Prea Ket Mealea*'s reign. Buddha *Khosa* left Ceylon between AD 430 and 440. But we know that he safely reached his country where he died old. (V. Barthelemy-St-Hilaire)

The discovering of the sudden decline of that unknown civilisation seems to emerge from the study of the Khmer monuments the degree of perfection of which is, after all, the only authentic evidence of this fabulous marvel which was totally unheard of just a few years ago. The edifice considered the most beautiful, Angkor Wat, is the least ancient. The strange monuments of *Bati, Battambang* and also *Phnom Bachey* (except for its restored central tower), all seem to be from the same era. If they are not as grandiose as those of Angkor, it is because the elite artists were in the capital and in the provinces the resources were limited. Next to these beautiful monuments and without transition one finds ordinary and unattractive modern constructions.

The inscriptions which have until now been deciphered, those of *Phnom Bachey* and *Bati*, for example, refer to a pious work the memory of which they retain. They have nothing in common with the construction of the monument, and only demonstrate its veneration. The tradition, which we must resort to for want of anything better, seems to confirm the hypothesis of this sudden and total fall, by attributing it to the curse cast onto the kingdom as a punishment for a crime of *Sdach Komlong*.

A long time after *Prea Ket Mealea*, there reigned a king who, having become leprous, was nicknamed *Sdach Komlong* (the leprous king). The *Maha Rosey* (*maha rischis*, the great Anachorete), very virtuous, pitied him and sent one of his disciples to look after him and cure him. This disciple, after having seen

Statue of the leper king in Angkor Thom, 1870, MAE

The restored statue is now on display at the
National Museum of Cambodia in Phnom Penh.

the king, considered the cure difficult and declared: "If the king wants to be cured and regain his beauty and his health, he must let me resurrect him." And since the king did not believe him, he added that he was going to test his power straight away. He boiled some water in a big basin, threw a dog alive into it and cooked it until it was completely disintegrated; then, he added certain powders into the basin and the dog reappeared beautiful and full of life. He then invited the king to step into the basin, promising him that he too would come out handsome and healthy. The king replied that he could not reconcile himself to it since he was not yet convinced. So the disciple offered to go into the basin and he gave the king three types of powder, saying: "This one, you add it when the cooking is done; it will give me back my human form. Then you throw in this other type which will bring me back my beauty, and finally the third one will bring me back my intelligence and life."

And so he stepped into the basin. But the king, instead of following the order prescribed, threw in the three types of powder at the same time. The *Maha Rosey*'s disciple in the basin was turned into a stone statue which the leprous king threw onto the neighboring mountain. This statue had a *chrakreng* posture (the arms and legs were tucked and s*prea*d). And since that time, the mountain kept the name of *Phnom Bakeng*. The *Maha Rosey*, who had fixed a deadline of seven days with his disciple, seeing that he was not returning, feared the worst and headed for the palace. Having heard what had happened, in his holy anger he got hold of a stick with which he grooved a stone in the courtyard of the palace, cursing the kingdom of the *Sdach Komlong*, dooming it to misfortune and decadence and concluding in these words: "May that kingdom become prosperous again only the day this stone will, by itself, manage to level out its groove." Then he went to Mount Bakeng, resurrected his disciple and took him back into the forest *Hem Baupeen* (*hem, hima*, cold, winter).

Be that as it may of this terrible curse, it is a fact that there is not one population presenting a contrast as striking as the Khmer, degenerated nowadays from the Khmer from the past as it is revealed by these grandiose ruins, before which the melancholic description which Mouhot borrows from P. Bouillevaux (*Voyage dans l'Indo-Chine*) is constantly brought back to mind: "Comparing the different shades erased by the night in the scenery, to that of the life of the populations when glory and hope cease to give it the magic of their colors."

Finally, we will report another tradition relating the first defeat of this power.

Long after *Prea Ket Mealea*, the Khmer king, who was reigning in Angkor, there was *Bautumo Saurivong* (whom one must not mistake for the founder of Angkor). His eyes were endowed with a supernatural force. It was under this king that the Khmer country fell into decline and that the predominance of Siam became prominent. A predestined man, *Ponhea Roung*, was born in Siam (*Ponhea* is a title of little importance, *Roung* is the *Phra Ruang* of the Siamese, who was, so the legend says, of mediocre extraction). Still a child, he took the religious habit, and as a disciple he stayed in the pagoda of Wat Pour.

At that time, the inhabitants of Siam were compelled, twice a month, to carry water in lead vases, either for drinking of for bathing, to *Beautumo Saurivong*. This water was drawn from the lake of *Kras Ngoli*.

One day, the *Ponhea Roung* saw some Siamese pass by and asked them whom this water was for. From their answer that it was for the Khmer king, he guessed that in this kingdom there was the man with supernatural eyes. But he remained silent.

Some time later, the Siamese, exasperated by the duty which they were forced into, revolted and their army went all the way to Siem Reap.[1] Warned by his mandarins, *Bautumo Saurivong* gave orders to have his elephants prepared to take him to the Siamese army. Within sight of this army, his eyes scanned it and made it flee without the Siamese being able to fight back. As soon as his supernatural eyes fixed a group of people, an army corps, the Siamese in that group, terrorised, ran away and scattered all over.

Defeated, the Siamese continued to carry the water until the day *Ponhea Roung*, whose words had supernatural power, was sixteen years old.

Then he ordered the Siamese to chop down bamboos, cleave them, make *phnek kruoch* baskets with them (small simple wide-meshed baskets, used for containing eggs, fruit, etc...) and to use these baskets to carry the water for *Bautumo Saurivong*. The latter, at the sight of this miracle, cried: "A man with a great supernatural power is born in Siam! Siam will flourish."

He [*Ponhea Roung*] summoned his mandarins, repeated these words and added: "From now on, the Khmers are destined to obey the Siamese. Therefore, make sure you order them and impose some duty onto them!"

This is the single and only time the *Ponhea Roung* asked the water to be fetched and carried in those baskets. Afterwards he forbid the Siamese to obey the Khmers.

In the Khmer kingdom, a grand mandarin, the *Oknha Dechou Ahksena*, called *Kraham Ka* (Red-Neck), extremely brave, was second to none to fight in a war. Realizing that the Siamese were not fulfilling their duty as they did before, he went and bowed in front of his king, begging for his authorisation to gather an army to punish them. "Be careful not to do so, said the

---

1 The present administrative centre of the province of Angkor, a few kilometres south of this point. The name of Siem Reep which still remains could be literally translated by the trivial expression: flattened Siamese.

Bas-relief at Angkor Wat, 1866, MAE

king. In the kingdom of Siam was born a man with supernatural words; you will not defeat him". The *Oknha Dechou*, a grand mandarin, proud of the supernatural power he himself had, that is to walk underground, did not listen to his king and gathered some men whom he took to the kingdom of Siam. Three walking days away from the pagoda where the *Ponhea Roung* was staying, he asked his army to stop and he continued on his own, going deep underground. Close to the pagoda, the upper half of his body springing up, he shouted: "Where are you, *Oknha Dechou*?" "I heard that you have been gifted with a great power thanks to your supernatural mouth, and I have gathered an army so that we can fight." The *Ponhea Roung* replied: "Enough! Why fight? You've come all this way, stay where you are! And your men over there, they aren't moving either!" The *Oknha* remained with half his body underground and died in that position. Also and until their death all the soldiers were immobilized where they were standing when the *Ponhea Roung* spoke.

Siam became free and flourishing under *Ponhea Roung*. The Khmer kingdom with *Bautumo Saurivong,* continued to be in a state of decline, but it was not under Siam's domination yet.

From this relatively modern legend, taking the miracles into account, one can extract a few historical outlines.  The Khmer king suppressed a first insurrection by the Siamese, a formidable insurrection since it had taken them to the gates of Angkor.  The Siamese having in their legendary liberator found a chief worthy of them, *Bautumo Saurivong* grew weary of trying to crush them.  One of his dignitaries, more energetic, wanted to pursue the fight, but, without support, he was probably caught in an ambush and his death was followed by the massacre of his army.

In order to explain this big reversal of fortune, the Khmer pride  has the supernatural, which in this naive people replaces the term equally convenient for treason and those  reserved for small democracies and the inconsequental.

Phnom Bachey near the Mekong, 1867-1875, MAE

# 3 - HISTORICAL PAST

The Khmer did not recover from the blow dealt by the Siamese who had become their fierce enemies. For a long time, the city of Angkor remained the capital, well fallen without doubt, and too much exposed to the more and more insistent Siamese incursions. Finally, in the 15th Century the kings of Cambodia abandoned it and moved to the opposite end of the Lake, to *Babaur*, in the east of the province of *Pursat*. The official Royal Chronicle, a dry compilation of dates and royal titles constantly repeated, translated under the direction of Mr. de Lagrée, gives a poor idea of the increasingly miserable state of that country. In the 16th Century, moving even further away from Siam, these princes settled southeast of *Babaur* in *Lovek*, where they built a large citadel surrounded by an impenetrable forty-meter wide bamboo forest. This natural wall did not prevent the citadel from being taken, according to the tradition thanks to a simple stratagem. The Siamese, by way of projectiles, threw gold and silver coins into the fence and left. In order to collect them, the Cambodians cleared the area by cutting down the bamboos. And so the Siamese came back to overtake the citadel. But, this tradition does not say much about the savage act attributed by the Siamese annals to the conqueror *Phra Naret*.

Full of fury against the King of Cambodia who had attacked him in the middle of a painful long fight against the *Pegou*, *Phra Naret* is said to have pledged to wash his feet in his enemy's blood, and to have kept his word. The Cambodians who are aware of this version got it from a Siamese and say that their own traditions have remained silent on this matter.

Following this disaster and after numerous journeys, the Khmer kings settled in *Oudong*, between *Lovek* and *Phnom Penh*, the current capital, which, in fact, welcomed them several times.

But a new neighbor, even more dangerous than the Siamese was rising in the East: the *Giao Chi*, the most tenacious and vigorous race in Indochina who had had their cradle in *Tonkin*. Bounded on the east by the sea, stopped in the west by mountains and almost impenetrable forests, and in the north by the homogenous and superior mass of people in the Celestial Empire, they quickly expanded to the south, absorbing or completely displacing a population of Malaysian origin, the *Chams*, the inhabitants of the *Champa* of Marco Polo. In the middle of 17th Century, they found themselves in contact with the Cambodians who were occupying the delta of the great river and the western side of the Cochin-chinese mountain chain. Bring the war to the heart of Cambodia, treat its kings as vassals, colonise *Bien Hoa* and Saïgon with Annamese and Chinese people, support a gang of Chinese adventurers thrown into the wild as lost children in *Hatien*, in the gulf of Siam have *Vinh Long* given to them and colonise it, appoint a viceroy in Saïgon in order to look after those vast possessions, occupy the remaining parts of the mouths of the river, go up north and establish themselves all the way to *Chaudoc, take Banteey Meas, Kampot* and *Kompong Som.*[1]

From then on the ancient Kampouchea was nothing but the stakes of the rivalry between the Siamese and the Annamese, who sometimes fought each other directly and sometimes fostered a civil war by supporting ambitious and rival princes which Cambodia was never short of. In such a miserable situation, the fields were abandoned, the country was almost like a desert, people were so unhappy that the old practices which they were most attached to were being lost. Even Buddhism was distorted by rituals which rightly are regarded as odious today. Blushing, he admitted, for example, that the young men who

---

1 These last three provinces were returned by *Tu Duc* in 1848), that is to say of the entire maritime coastline of Cambodia, this is what the Annamese achieved from 1658 to 1758.

were to join a religious order had the right, for three days, to openly and with impunity pursue the young ladies they fancied.

The Siamese invasions were the most devastating. According to the system of the ancient and barbaric Asian politics, these cruel conquerors transported far away, just like dirty herds, the inhabitants whom, fortunately, they did not slaughter. Little did they care about the sufferings and the miseries which killed almost all of these poor people during the journey. We must now go to Siam to collect the manuscripts, the legends, the satras, the traditions which were not destroyed. Statues, monuments, everything which could not be carried away was broken, damaged with ferocious rage accompanied by an instinct of destruction. The bitter memory of past servitude plus the savage belief that with these noble remains, which were objects of respect and unconscious veneration, the ancient spirit of a whole people and their hope to find happiness again, that is the prosperity that they required from the works of their wonderful ancestors, would be shattered.

The Annamese, with less cruelty but with more reliability and rapidity, were getting rid of the conquered people. Their invader's mind, assisted by the tax genius of their administrators, probably applied the same system which had been very successful in *Champa* with an equal success. Mocked, despised, systematically frustrated, the Cambodians were severely punished when, running out of patience, they took their revenge through barbarian acts which are the natural and true result of their exasperation. At the beginning of this century, they had completely disappeared from *Bienhoa* and Saïgon; twenty or thirty years later from *Tanan, Gocong, Bentre* and *Mocay*. The French conquest arrived just in time, not to put an end but to delay the assimilation of those who had settled in *Tra Vinh* and *Soctrang* (*Bassac*).

At the end of the 18th Century, right in the middle of the

revolt of *Tay Son,* Cambodia had been conquered all the way to the Lake.  Nevertheless, the Siamese, already occupiers of vast Cambodian territories, took advantage of the troubles in Annam to lay their hands on Battambang and Angkor.  For his part, *Gia Long,* strengthened on his throne, increased the predominance of the Annamese influence to the extent of reducing *Ang Chan* to a complete state of vassalage and dependance.  The revolt of the Siamese partly resulted from this and, obviously, the blood princes joined it.  The governor of *Kompong Soa*i, the *Dechou Min*g, forced to flee to Siam, by his own authority gave away the provinces of *Tonle Repou* and *Melu Prey*, situated in the north of Cambodia in the middle basin of the Mekong River (1810).

When *Ang Chan* died (1832), the Annamese, encouraged by success, tried to take over the whole of Cambodia, but they were driven out by indigenous people with the help of the Siamese.  Following a struggle which was a combination of success and setbacks, the two powers acknowledged King *Ang Duong* (1846) who seemed to accept the status of dual vassal of the kingdoms vis-à-vis Siam and Annam, which were officially described as father and mother of Cambodia.

This truce would cease at the death of *Ang Duong* (1860).  The opportunities to have a civil war break out have not have been lacking.  The common objective was the total possession of the Lake and its fisheries.  The final outcome, more or less delayed, could be doubtful.  The Annamese were asserting themselves in the delta, the population of which was rapidly increasing.  To this population of boatmen the river provided a way for an easy and convenient invasion, but an unexpected new force came onto the scene.

France, by taking over the mouths of the river, stopped the conquering march of the Annamese.  It freed Cambodia from the Siamese claims by convincing a smart and clever prince [Norodom], who liked the Europeans, to accept its protection. Later on, unfortunately, Siam realising that France was maintaining its domination in Indochina, lost all hopes of expanding in Cambodia, and, as a wise and well-advised neighbor, thought about having its possession of the rich province of Battambang recognised by the French government, as well as the province of Angkor which contains the wonderful ruins of the old capital. In exchange, Siam was promising the abandon-

The pagoda of the queen mother, the wife of Ang "Duong, at Oudong, 1866-1875, MAE

ment of its right of suzerainty over Cambodia, a so-called right which the simple fact of our power in lower Cochinchina had already reduced to nothing. French diplomacy in 1867 obligingly ratified the pillaging of these two provinces and, therefore, the sharing of the domination of the Lake and the lower basin of the Mekong [The French-Siamese Treaty of 1867]. The Siamese kept silent about the two provinces of *Tonle Repou* and *Melu Prey* which they had received from the hands of a rebel governor. This easy acquisition, although coming after that of Battambang and Angkor, up till now was never ratified by any treaty with Cambodia.[1]

Battambang, 1867-1875, KMV

---

1 See the *Gia Dinh Thung Chi* (translation by Aubaret); *le Voyage d'exploration au Mekong* (Garnier); *la Chronique royale du Cambodge* (Garnier). This author is wrong when he says that *Truong Niuh Giang* ordered the killing of Ang Mey. This princess, still alive today, lives in Oudong.

## 4 - THE CURRENT STATE - VARIOUS RACES

The Kingdom of Cambodia today stretches between 101° 30' and 104° 30' east of the meridian of Paris and 10° 30' and 14° north latitude. Limited in the southwest by the gulf of Siam, it has as neighbors in the southeast French Cochinchina; in the northeast, some of the tribes which live in the forests of the Cochinchinese mountain chain; in the north, Laos, *Tonle Repou* and *Melu Prey*; in the northwest and in the west, Angkor and Battambang. It forms a slightly long rectangle from the northeast to the southwest. The longer part is more than 400 kilometres, from the point south of *Kompong Som* to *Stung Treng*, where the river exits Laos. The larger width of the western boundary of the province of *Pursat* to the eastern boundary of *Svai Teep* is about 300 kilometres. The area is more than 100.000 square kilometres.

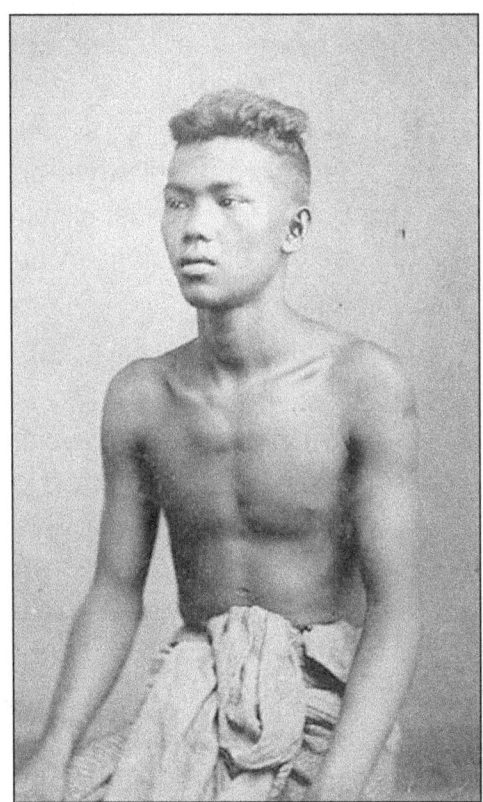

A Cambodian man, 1866-1875, KMV

The population, estimated at one million souls at the most, gives ten inhabitants per square kilometre. It mainly occupies the banks of the Mekong. These banks could be even more populated and make this river a huge route inhabited all along. There are rich cultures of betel, cotton, mulberry trees and indigo which constitute a notable income for the Cambodian government. The interior of the country, not very much inhabited, bears traces of devastation everywhere. In the past, even in living memory, Cambodia, which was populated and cultivated, was covered with numerous fruit-trees. The war got rid of the trees and the people.

Without taking into account one hundred thousand Cambodians scattered over our Cochinchinese possessions, the Khmer race, besides the present kingdom of Cambodia, populates Battambang, Angkor, *Tonle Repou, Melu Prey, Souren, Koukan* and all the way to *Korat* (*Angkor Reach Sema*). One can evaluate the number of people speaking its language at 1,500,000 over an area larger than the third of France.

A Cambodian woman, 1866-1875, KMV

Besides the native people, that is to say, as far as we know, the Khmers, the *Samre*, and the *Kouys*, Cambodia is populated by several races from which we are going to digress slightly before continuing on our topic.

1 - The Malays (*Chvea*) and the *Chams*. These two groups of Malaysian origin tend to merge, or rather the *Chams*, losing their originality, are being absorbed by the Malays every day. If the language of the *Chams* evidentially indicates their origin, it presents notable

differences with that of the Malays which is only a simple dialect of Malaysia.

The religion shared by everyone is the 'mohametism' of the Sunni sect. Several Malays make the pilgrimage to Mecca and return as hadjis. By reputation they know Constantinople (Istanbul) and the Sultan. It is worth noting that numerous traditions, particularly in the southeastern part of Cambodia, seem to attest to a *Cham* domination which may have taken place in a very distant past. It would be interesting to study this group where it has managed to stay pure of any similar influence, that is to say among groups which undoubtedly stayed in the old *Champa*, today forming the southern provinces of Annam.

The number of Malays and *Chams* can be estimated at about thirty thousands in Cambodia. They are spread over about fifty very dispersed villages, from *Kampot* to the *Tonle Sap* and on the big river from *Tonle Sap* to the rapids. In the kingdom they have often occupied positions of mandarins and often caught their share of the troubles that have torn the country.

As good Muslims the Malays give their daughters only to their co-religionists, and have the wives whom they choose outside their religion embrace it. Less apathetic than the Cambodians, they are harsher on their slaves.

2 - The Chinese. There are more than one hundred thousand sons of the Celestial Empire in Cambodia, where, like everywhere else, they have the reputation of being 'very useful' because they sustain a trade which would not exist without them. One should add that they are even perhaps more harmful, for want of a rational administrative system adopted and strictly respected with regard to them. They drain the cash and export it to China. In Cambodia, like everywhere else in fact, they are arrogant, corrupted or cringing depending on

the weakness, the corruption or the firmness of the authorities.

3 - Even more numerous soon will be the Annamese, who instinctively carry on their task of integration, eating into the borders, entering via the rivers, penetrating by all the streams. An Annamese wanders everywhere his junk goes, supporting with his natural philosophy the demands of a race for which he feels nothing but an instinctive aversion mingled with despisement. He retaliates by trying to continually fool the Cambodian with whom he forms the biggest contrast, except concerning a passion for gambling which both have in common. Having run out of resources, he pawns his wife, his children, his friends and, last, commits himself. Everywhere, outside of his own country, in part scornful or interested, but also with some indisputable truth, he shows a certain sympathy for the French whom he regards almost as his fellow countryman.

Cambodian girls,
1866-1875, KMV

4 - Persons of mixed race. Many Sino-Cambodians take after both races, after the Chinese if they are rich, after the Cambodian if they are from the low class.

The young ladies are relatively pretty and have a nice figure. They wear the Cambodian narrow sheath dress and the *langouti* falling onto their feet.

There are also many mixed Cambodian-Annamese people, although in less great number.

Other mixed race people have left behind interesting great-grandchildren in a small colony of Portuguese descendants. They keep the family names, but the very last of them who could speak the language of *Camoëns* died a few years ago. Physically they can be mistaken for the other Cambodians, among whom they are more or less the only Catholics. The conversions to Catholicism of the Khmers, who are avid Buddhists, are very rare, and not really sincere; they are always done out of self-interest.

A group of cambodian children, 1866-1875, KMV

King Norodom of Cambodia in 1866, MAE

# 5 - THE KING

The government of Cambodia is an absolute monarchy. The king is the only Master, the one and only owner of the kingdom. He appoints and removes the great mandarins and the governors of the provinces as he pleases. He sets the taxes, he makes the laws; he is the supreme magistrate. Everything goes back to him and follows from him. One single exception is made for the clergy, for religion; true Buddhism, practised in Cambodia, does not admit the interference of either the secular power in the cult or that of the clergy in politics.

Usually the king is the eldest prince of a very old royal family (*Prea Vongsa*). Before ascending the throne, he will have occupied royal dignities which we will talk about later. The Cambodians have several expressions to name him. The most common ones are *luong* and *sdach*. In a more precise and respectful manner, they also say *luong mechas chivit*, the *luong* master of lives, or *luong trong reech*, the governing *luong*. He is also given one or several other titles which he took when ascending the throne.

The current king, who had been a prince for forty years, resides in Phnom Penh (the full mountain).[1] His palace is a wide enclosed area, comprising several groups of buildings. Across it, a wall divides it in two parts: the public and official part, and the residential part, reserved for the women. These women,

---

1 This name comes from the fact that it stands on an artificial mound, a huge and dense pile of bricks, as its name suggests. On this mound stands a pyramid (chay dey), the conical and slender top of which can be seen from far away. The construction of this pyramid must be dating from a distant past, but later than the construction of the big monuments, at least as far as the style is concerned. Big and strong trees have grown on the layer of soil which now covers the brick mound. According to Mr. De Lagrée, the mound is 27 meters high and the monument 32.

about two or three hundred of them, are in several social categories depending on their birth; there are princesses, daughters of grand or lower mandarins, or of ordinary people. Among themselves there is a certain hierarchy inside which they can go up in privileges and honors depending either on the mood of the master or favors done; among these, the most appreciated is the denouncing of unfaithfulness.

When a prince ascends the throne or occupies a royal dignity, it is customary in Cambodia just like in other Asian countries, not to call him by his name anymore. The name, in fact, is only used for ordinary people, never for dignitaries. If the name of the king is a word of the common language, something quite common in Cambodia, this word is often changed. And so, for *Ang Duong*, the word *Duong*, which means a small coin, has been replaced by the word *dom*.

Just like for his predecessors, in 1864 when the current king celebrated the ceremony (*aphisek*) which replaces the crowning of the western despots, the learned members (*acha*) of the court prepared and submitted a list of royal titles taken from the *Pali*. He is officially named by all these titles in the important acts, and by a few only in the ordinary documents.

They are: *Prea Bat Samdach Prea Noroudam Baromma Reama Tevatana Kunnasa Santhorit Mahe Savara Thuppedey Serey Saurionvong Norapatthapong Damrang Reas Baromma Neeth Maha Kampouchea Thuppedintho Sappasellapa Presathi Satthat Satha Por Prumma Mer Amnoi Chey Chea Mahe Savaria Thuppedey Ey Patha Pidol Sokala Kampouchea Nachakk Aka Maha Baras Raht Vivattha Nea Terek Ek Andam Barommahapit Prea Chau Krong Ea Thuppedey Chea Ammechas Chivit Loeuh Thbaung.*

And here follows their translation which, in fact, in order to be accurate, should go back to the sanskrit etymology:

Holy Feet, The Lord, Glorious Among People, Perfect, Rama, Descendant of Celestial Spirits, Incomparable and

King Norodom of Cambodia in 1866, MAE

Sublime Merit, Supreme Arbitrator, Gracious Son Of The Sun, Absolute Essence Of Humanity, Leader Of People, Supreme Refuge, Regulator of the Grand Kampouchea, Omniscient, Almighty, Eternal Beauty, Who Received Victory and Immortality As a Gift From Brahma, Supreme Arbitrator of The Kingdom, Power Which Spreads Over All Kampouchea, Superb and Magnificent Man, Diamond Being the Source of Prosperity, Unique Splendor, Noble and Sublime Prince, Eminent and Divine Arbitrator of the Capital of Kampouchea, Master of Lives Placed Above All the Heads.

The Khmers grant their king what we Europeans extend to our Majesties, Highnesses, Eminences, Lordships, etc..., etc.

From Noroudam, the French came up with the name Norodom.

For a few years now, His Cambodian Majesty has had the title *Norapatthapong* changed into *Maha Chahk Patthapong*, the descendant of the grand *Chahk Path* (*Tchakravarti*, the king of the Wheel).[1]

The king is the supreme judge. Whoever thinks they must complain about a denial of justice can come to him directly. One of the royal chief officers (*Chankrom Prea Damrnot*) is responsible for examining the complaint and informing the king who then decides. The persons who ask for justice to be done expose themselves to a serious punishment if the complaint is not founded. It can reach the king in two different ways called, *rong deyka* and *sar tuhk*. The *rong deyka* consists in turning up at the palace at the time the king is granting an audience and in asking a guard to strike a few beats on a '*tamtam*' drum; the guard receives four 'ligatures' [a measure of money] per beat. The king sends a page to collect the complaint. The *sar tuhk* takes place when the plaintiff bows when the king walks past

---

[1] This expression designates the princes who, in various eras of humanity, have to exercise a universal domination (A. Remusat, *Melanges Posthumes*).

and he keeps holding his written complaint above his head until the king picks it. This last procedure which does not cost anything is more commonly used than the *rong deyka*.

The Queen of Cambodia, 1866, MAE

The king's half-brother, Sisowath, 1865-1867, MAE

# 6 - DIGNITARIES - SAMRAP

The kingdom's high dignitaries also have pompous *Pali* titles, more or less numerous depending on their dignity. To make things simple we will only name them by their more commonly used title. All these dignities, as well as the provinces in the kingdom, are divided in four big categories called *samrap*. One can tell the difference between the *samrap* by their cardinal numbers in *Pali*: *ek, tou, trey, chetva* (one, two, three, four).

- The king is the natural head of the *samrap ek*.
- The *samrap tou* is reserved to the king who abdicated, *luong obbaioureech*. (Abdications often took place in the history of Cambodia)
- The *samrap trey* to the first prince of the blood, *samrap* or *luong maha, obbarach*.
- The *samrap chetva* to the first princess of the blood; *samdach prea teau*.

At the moment, there is no *obbaioureech*; the king has kept to himself the privileges of this royal dignity. He could, following numerous precedents, give the *samrap tou* to the *obbarach* and the *samrap trey* to a second prince who would have the title *prea keo fa*. So, under Ang Duong the eldest son, the current king, was *obbarach* with the *samrap tou,* and the current *obbarach* was *Prea Keo fK* and already had the *samrap trey*.

The *samrap chetva* is naturally reserved to the king's mother, if she is still alive, as is the case today. This princess then has the title *luong* or *Samdach Prea Voreechini* (*samdach*, lord; *prea*, divine; *vora*, beautiful; *reech*, royal; *chini*, mother).

The numerous dignitaries of each *samrap* are called mandarins by the Europeans, the same name as the civil servants of China. In the Khmer language they are called *nomoeun* or *namoeun*, or *namoeun nacen*, an expression which is an alteration of *moeun*, ten thousand; *sen*, one hundred thousand or *muhk montrey*. Everything which is not *namoeun* is *reas* (ordinary person, from the common people).

In each *samrap*, the mandarins are classified from top to bottom in ten categories of *sahk* (dignities, honors), that can be distinguished between them by the number of thousands, *pahn*, or by alteration, *hupahn*. This word, therefore, here expresses a kind of very particular unity.

And so one will say: *namoeun sahk dap pahn*, mandarin with ten thousand dignities, *namoeun sahk pram bey pahn*, a mandarin with eight thousand dignities.

Those ranked highest have the title *samdach* with ten *pahn*. Then come the *oknha* with ten, nine, eight, seven or six *pahn*. - The *chauponhea* with six, five, four *pahn*, - the *prea* with six, five, four *pahn*, - the *luong* with four, three *pahn*, - the *khun* with three, two *pahn*, - the *moeun* with two *pahn*, one *pahn* five *roi* (hundreds), one *pahn*, - the *neey* with one *pahn* five roi, one *pahn*.

Prince Yukanthor, the Heir Apparent in 1866, KMV

And all the way to the village chiefs (*me sroh*) who have one thousand or five hundred dignities (*pram roi*) and their subordinates (*chumtup*), hamlet chiefs, who have a few hundred dignities and honors.

One regards the *samdach* and the *oknha* as grand mandarins; the others are small mandarins.

As for the honors and the rules of etiquette, the *samrap ek*, by far the most important, is regarded as superior by one degree to the *samrap tou*; so that a *namoeun sahk* eight *pahn samrap ek*, will go together with a *namoeun sahk* nine *pahn samrap tou*. Likewise, the *samrap tou* is one degree above the *samrap trey*, and the latter is above the *samrap chetva*.

The attributions of the corresponding dignities in the various *samrap* are similar, but cannot be mistaken for one another. A mandarin of any *samrap* is not, in principle, the subordinate of the mandarin who has the same dignity in a superior *samrap*. It is by mistake to claim that under the orders of the *Kralahom* are placed the *Pibol*, who is the *Kralahom samrap tou*, and the *Bautes* who is the *Kralahom samrap trey*.

There being an equal number of *samrap* and *sahk*, the mandarins of the crown, or, according to the Cambodian expression, the mandarins of the interior (na*moeun kenong*), are superior to those of the provinces, or the exterior (na*moeun* krau).

Often, in a single *samrap*, two equal mandarins have the same functions which they either alternate with one another or share the area; in this case they are distinguished by the qualifications of left (*chhveng*) and right (*sedam*).

A Cambodian Princess,
1866-1875, KMV

An uncle of the king,
1866, KMV

A Cambodian Minister, 1866-1875, MAE,

# 7 - MANDARINS OF THE INTERIOR

Here are the main mandarins of the interior of the various *samrap*; we will list them by their most commonly used titles.

## SAMRAP EK

Above all the mandarins of the kingdom, he is a kind of viceroy whose title can change, whose dignity is not regular. This first dignitary today bears the title of *Samdach Prea Ang Kev*. Under previous reigns he was called *Prea Changveang*. Often this viceroyalty was not occupied; therefore the first mandarin is the *Samdach Chaufea*, a kind of suzerain prime minister (*Chaufai Kamnan*) of the provinces of the land of *Kampong Soai*. The *Chaufea* is sometimes call *Khmang Pos* (back of a snake). The same person, a 76 year old man, is currently *Prea Ang* and *Chaufea*.

Then there are:

The *Oknha Joumreech*, grand justiciary of the *samrap ek*, taking care of the thieves and the murderers, and suzerain of the provinces of *Treang*.

The *Oknha Veang*, grand majordomo, treasurer for the royal magazine and the palace, and suzerain of *Thhaung Khmum*.

The *Oknha Kralahom*, responsible for the royal transportation by junks, for the royal marine (the current king reserves the right to keep an eye on his steamers); The *Kralahom* is suzerain of *Ba Phnom*.

The *Oknha Chakrey*, responsible for the royal transportation by land, of the elephants, the bulls, the buffaloes, the horses, the carriages, and also suzerain of *Pursat*. The dignitary who, at the moment, carries out the functions of *Chakrey* has the special title of *Presor Saurivong* (illustrious descendant of the sun).

These four dignities, collectively designated by the words *Chado Sedam*, the four columns (of the empire), or by *Choeung Krus*, which stems from *krus* (old vase with four stems), with the

*Chaufea* to form the five mandarins of the interior with ten *pahn* of the *samrap* ek. They are the five most important mandarins of the kingdom.

Then there are:

The *Oknha Maha Muntrey*, the *Oknha Maha Tep*, the two chamberlains on the right and on the left who introduce the mandarins at the king's audience.

The *Oknha Pitheak Eysora* and the *Oknha Reaksa Eysora* with several mandarins under their orders guard and serve the king inside his palace.

The *Oknha Maha Sena* and the *Oknha Jouthea Sangkreem* are two vanguard commanders who walk in front of the king during a war.

The *Oknha Sauphea Thuppedey* and the *Oknha Muntrey Ketdarach*, two royal judges who decide on all the causes which are brought in front of them, or which they have been entrusted with by the king.

The eight preceding *muntrey* are nine *pahn*; they walk behind the *Chado Sedam*.

The *Oknha Akarea Chenda* is the chief of the royal secretaries' corps (*alahk*);

The *Oknha Vongsa Thuppedey* and the *Oknha Serey Thubes Reachea* supervise the list of the registered population. These two mandarins bearing the collective name *Serey Sauriodey* (or commonly, by alteration, *Suos Dey*) receive the money coming from the buying back of duties, or command duties.

The *Oknha Kosa Thuppedey* and the *Oknha Prea Khleang Thuppedey* have the surveillance of the stores containing the metals (iron, copper, lead).

The *Oknha Dar Neiok* and the *Oknha Reachneiok* have the surveillance of the clothing stores and the wardrobe of the palace.

The *Oknha Pipheak Saley* are the *Oknha Pohuletep* are the two store men for the paddy.

The *Oknha Phimuk Muntrey* and The *Oknha Srey Akreech* are responsible for the rice store.

These eleven *Oknha* with eight *pahn* obey the *Oknha Veang*.

The *Oknha Auten* and the *Oknha Kuchenneyok* with eight *pahn*, with a lot of mandarins with seven and six *pahn*, are in charge of the surveillance of the elephants, the horses, the carriages, etc..., under the orders of the *Chakrey*.

The *Oknha Dechouchey*, the *Oknha Muntrey Sena*, the *Oknha Serey Nokobal* with seven *pahn*, the *Chau Ponhea Seren Trea*, the *Chau Ponhea Piphea Thebes*, the *Chau Ponhea Reem Dechou*, the *Chau Ponhea Menou Sena* with six *pahn* are in charge of the surveillance of the thieves, of the prisons under the orders of the *Joumreech*.

For the service of the junks, the *Kralahom* commands the *Oknha Tep Norchun*, the *Chau Ponhea Seren Cheey*, the *Chau Ponhea Phey Antrea*, etc., etc.

## SAMRAP TOU

The *Chaufea* of this *samrap* bears the title *Samdach Chau Ponhea*.

The *Oknha Vongsa Akreech*, the *Oknha Serey Thomea Thireech*, the *Oknha Vibol* or *Pibol Reech*, the *Oknha Reech Daychea* respectively are the *Joumreech*, the *Veang*, the *Kralahom*, the *Chakrey* of this *samrap*, all equally with ten *pahn*.

Then there is a whole hierarchy similar to the previous one. And so the *Oknha Nearea Thireach* and the *Oknha Sauphea Muntrey* are the two royal judges of this *samrap*. The *Oknha Presor Aksar* is the *Akara Chenda*.

The current *Presor Aksar* is the descendant of a Portuguese man known by the name of 'Col of Monteiro.'

The *Oknha Reachea Thubes* is the mandarin *Suos Dey* (registers of taxes), etc., etc.

## SAMRAP TREY

The *Khnang Pos* of this *Samrap* bears the title *Samdach Chetha*.

The *Chado Sedam* are: the *Oknha Ekarach*, the *Oknha Serey Sautupphuveang*, the *Oknha Bautes Reech*, the *Oknha Nearin Trea Thuppedey*. The *Oknha Thireech Muntrey* is the chamberlain. The royal judges are the *Oknha Sauphea Thireech* and the *Oknha Reachea Sauphea*, etc., etc. They all have the same number of *pahn* as their respective colleagues in the other *samrap*.

## SAMRAP CHETVA

We feel it is unnecessary to list the mandarins of this not very important *samrap*. It is a quintuple hierarchy equally copied from that of the *samrap ek*. These mandarins reside in Oudong, close to the queen mother.

We will conclude this long enumeration in adding that the main mandarins of each *samrap*, such as the *Chado Sedam*, are appointed and revoked by the king. For the others, this is done by the head of the *samrap*.

A Cambodian mandarin, 1866-1875, KMV

# 8 - PUOK OR KROM

Under the orders of several of these mandarins there are corps, corporations called *puok* or *rom* in Cambodian. We will talk about those of the *samrap ek*; they are reduced to very few in the other *samrap*.

1 - *The Puok Kromoveang* - In charge of the supervision of the women of the palace, on their own among all the *puok*, they serve in the private part. They are under the high guidance of the *Oknha Veang*, then of the *Thomea* or *Veang Samrap Tou*, finally of the *Esserea Noreak*, the *Serey Tupnet* and the *Reachea Tupnet*.

2 - The *Krom* of the *Maha Lek Anhchunh Kruong* - That is to say the corps of the pages responsible (when the king travels) for carrying the royal implements: the boxes containing the tobacco, the arek, the betel, the wick, and the royal clothes which are presented by the women. Under the high guidance of the *Presor Saurivong*, their chiefs are the *Luong Nai* and the *Prea Nai*.

3 - The *Krom Maha Lek Anhchunh Prea Seng* - The pages who accompany the king and carry the royal arms. At the time of the ceremony of drinking the water of the oath, they carry the royal arms to the pagoda where the ceremony takes place, and hand them over to the *Bakou*. In order to supervise their service, they have *Neey Ven* and *Balat Ven*.

4 - The *Krom Prea Damruot* - They are officers among who some carry bundles and walk in front of the king; others, armed with spears, walk behind. With rods they hit anyone who exposes himself to punishment as the king passes by. The *Bava Rea Chea* is their chief, and underneath him are *Chau Krom, Balat Krom, Neey Ven* and *Balat Ven*.

5 - The *Puok Teaheen Khmer*, a corps of Cambodian soldiers, trained and dressed almost the European way, under the orders of a *Chang Veang Teaheen* and of *Chau Krom, Balat Krom,*

*Chau Ven* and *Balat Ven*. Some guard the doors of the palace, others are in charge of firing the cannon, others are on secondment at the service of the navy which consists of five or six small steamers. Almost all these warriors are slaves who have been bought back ad hoc by the king and they have so little talent for the military service that not many days pass without desertions.

A Cambodian soldier, 1866-1875, KMV

6 - The *Puok Teaheen Manille*, *Tagals* who are engaged at the service of the king and maintain security in Phnom Penh and the city markets. Their chief, with the title *Luong Areak Reachea* is of mixed race, Spanish and Cambodian. His name is *don Pasquale de la Cruce*. Some *Tagals* form the corps of royal musicians, European style.

7 - The *Krom Teaheen Se Chea Cavalerie;* as its French name indicates, is a corps on horse back. It is composed of sons of mandarins and notables whom the king makes learn horse riding and horse handling. They are his escort. Their chiefs are *Achnha Darong Sena*. All these young men are members of *puok* number two of the pages, from which they are detached. *Puok* five, six and seven constitute the whole regular army of Cambodia, composed of between four and five hundred men. In wartime

or rebellion, the men among the population are mobilised and armed with sticks, swords and spears.

8 - The *Alahk*, or royal secretaries, have a chief, the *Alara Chenda,* and some *Balat Krom, Neey Ven* and *Balat Ven* to supervise the service. The *Alahk* collect and bring the taxes of all kind to the king, they write letters, royal orders and keep all the registers. Apart from the accounts of the *Alahk* there are only the records of the people who are registered and the money coming in from the buying back of duties (See note 14).

Every month the *Alahk* hand over the state of the income and expenses of the royal treasury to the *louk.*

In the past, just like the pages, they were under the orders of the *Chaufea.*

The eight *krom* previously mentioned are divided into shifts of service with a chief for each shift (*ven*).

The cavalry and the pages are paid an annual bonus, the *Teaheen* khmer earn monthly wages. The *Tagals* have a decent salary. The other *puok* are not paid anything.

To these main *krom* one can add:

9 - The *Puok Khleang Meniroht*, and

10 - The *Puok Khleang Kausey Phahs* who are the keepers of the stores for metals and those for clothes (wardrobe). They are under the high guidance of the *Louk Yeang,* to whom every month and through the *Alahk,* they hand over the state of credits and debits and what is left in the store. Through the same intermediary they receive the money for purchases.

11 - The various *puok* of the jewellers, goldsmiths, sculptors, metal and wood turners.

12 - The *Krom Reaksa Prea* Ang, the royal male servants. Many small mandarins compose this domestic staff. This *puok*, although it has kept its denomination, was replaced by the *dam-*

*ruot* in the king's personal staff. Today the *Raksa Pra Ang* supervise the workmen who work for the palace, or they are in charge of small missions outside the palace. Their chiefs are the *Pipheak Eysora* and the *Reaksa Eysora*.

13 - The *Krom Roung Pum Reech Montit*, the printers-lithographers. Their chiefs, the *Banha Thuppedey* and the *Santhar Reechena*, have laws, ordinances and the official printed gazette. When there is a trial before the judges, they have to communicate to them the text of the law in order to help them with the deciding of the sentence.

14 - The *Kom Hora*, the royal astrologists - The four of them, the *Oknha Tupechahk*, the *Reech Angre,* the *Visay Meianet* and the fourth one, who is without a title, are in charge of putting together the calendar, determining new year's day, the seasons, and the eclipses. Sometimes they read the horoscope and predict the future.

15 - The *Krom Teaheen Kan Tongchey Kraham*, the red standards bearers. The chiefs are: for the right wing (*Khang Sedam*), the *Oknha Maha Sena*; for the left wing (*Khang Chhveng*), the *Oknha Jouthea Sangkreem*; the two vanguard commanders who carry the red standard in front of the king. This *puok*, remanants of the Khmer army, are recruited from among the royal hereditary slaves (*pol, neahk ngear*).

16 - The *Krom Khleang Phouch Saley*, the store men for the paddy. The chiefs are the *Oknha Pohuletep* (*sedam*), the *Pipheak Saley* (*chhveng*). This *puok* receives the 'tax of paddy' and delivers it as needed by the palace.

17 - The *Krom Khleang Pouchnea*, storemen for the rice. The chiefs are the *Muhk Montrey* (*sedam*), the *Serey Akerech* (*chhveng*). When the rice is about to run out, it is delivered from

the paddy by the previous *puok*, and the rice of this paddy is husked by slaves (*pol*) destined to this job. The best rice is offered to the monks; the rest is used for the needs of the palace. All these store-men keep some record for their common chief, the *Louk Veang*.

18 - Finally, a last *puok* worthy of remark is the *Krom Prea Sangkrey*, whose chief is a mandarin with nine *pahn*, the *Oknha Prea Sdach Thuppedey*, with five or six mandarins lower in rank and under his orders. This *krom* sees to the religious side of all the festivities which take place at the palace; he invites the monks and prepares the throne room for them. Part of the duty of the *Prea Sdach* and his subordinates is to make sure that the special law, *Prea Reech Kret Sangkrey*, is observed. To this effect, in all the provinces, they have some permanent delegates (*phneak ngear*) who inflict condemnations for the offences infringing that law: offences perpetrated by the monks, by the laity towards the monks, and offences against the moral code.

A Cambodian elephant with a palanquin, 1866-1875, KMV

An important rich man, 1866-1875, MAE

# 9 - THE PROVINCES - EXTERIOR MANDARINS

According to several indications, the Khmer kingdom was previously divided into five large provinces under the suzerainty of five high officers of the crown. Each of them had a lieutenant mandarin with ten *pahn* at the head of their province. The governor of *Kompong Soai* with the title *Oknha Dechou* was the *Chaufea* of the exterior, and his government, besides the current province of *Kompong Soai*, comprised *Stung, Chikreng, Barai, Stung Trang*, etc. The *Joumreech* was represented by the *Oknha Pus Nulouk*, governor of the province of *Treang*, located between the Grand River and the sea. In *Thbaung Khmum*, on the grand River in the northeast, the *Oknha Archun* obeyed the *Oknha Veang*. In *Ba Phnom*, in the southeast, the *Oknha Thomea Dechou* was the lieutenant of the *Kralahom*. Finally in *Pursat* the *Suokealouk* paid tribute to the *Chakrey*.

In the central part of the kingdom, near Oudong and Phnom Penh, some small provinces served as privileges for other mandarins of the *Samrap Ek*, or by highly ranked mandarins of lower *samrap*.

This big division of the kingdom was already altered before Ang Duong. For example, *Bati* and *Prey Krebas* formed provinces distinct from *Treang*. The provinces, larger and less numerous than they are today, were administered by governors appointed by the king. Each province was subdivided in *muong* and had at their head a *Chau Muong* appointed by the governor. Ang Duong raised all these *muong* to the rank of provinces or *khet*, and named all the governors under the generic title of *chaufai* or *chaufai khet*.

The current king formed three or four new provinces, and today, in 1874, the kingdom is divided into fifty-six provinces, including forty-three of the *Samrap Ek*, five of the *Samrap Tou*, five of the *Samrap Trey* and three of the *Samrap Chetva*.

The old division of the kingdom is something which has remained in the language with the word *dey* (land). And so, the Cambodians say that, in the Khmer kingdom, there is the land of *Kompong Soai*, the land of *Pursat*, etc..., and that one must be careful not to confuse with the provinces (*khet*) which nowadays, have kept the names of these old lands of which they are no more than the center. These very same provinces have also kept the grand vassals, sometimes called by the old generic title, *Sdach Tranh*.

They are high ranked mandarins, the only ones outside who are with ten *pahn*. If normally and for administrative and tax purposes, all the governors deal directly with the crown, in the case of a war or a rebellion the *Sdach Tranh* give orders to the others who, as a matter of fact, show them great respect. Among the governors only these five high dignitaries have the right of life or death over people, a right which they in actual fact don't exercise because, usually, for the crimes of common law, all criminals are sent to Phnom Penh.

The limited scope of this Note does not allow us to list the provinces and to give details on each of them. Let us only say that the five high officers of the crown have kept their old suzerainty almost intact, at least in terms of extent. Instead of having only one lieutenant they give orders to several governors.

After the five *Sdach Tranh*, *oknha* with ten *pahn*, all the other governors are *Oknha* with nine, eight, seven or six *pahn*. Besides the generic title of *Chaufai*, each has a special title, traditional in their respective province, and by which they are officially called.

Above the governors, in order to watch and assist them, the current king placed some *Achnha Luong* (missi dominici). This type of appointment is not applied overall. Often two or three provinces have one of these civil servants in common; many provinces do not have any. These *Achnha Luong* are permanent. Later we will see that there are some temporary ones, entrusted with special missions.

To assist his administration, the governor has subordinates whom he appoints himself, or as the Cambodian expression has it, whom he feeds (*chanhchem*). The number of these civil servants, named by the generic title *Kromokar*, therefore, depends on the whim of the governor or on the interest he believes a Cambodian has in buying a title.

The *Kromokar* usually are: the *Balat*, a kind of lieutenant who assists the *Chaufai*; sometimes as well as the *Balat khet*, there is a *Balat Luong*, meaning that he is appointed by the king; the *Snang*, the same word designates the official and the district. Usually there are two *Snang* distinguished by left and right (*chhveng, sedam*). Underneath there may be some *Preas* or *Kralapeas*, for inferior subdivisions. There may also be some *Chamtup Chaufai, Krai Suos, Osa, Prea Chuoy*, etc., etc.

Finally, at the bottom of the ladder there is the village (*srok*), the head of which (*me srok*) may have some subordinates (*chumtup*) at the head of the hamlets (*phum*). A *me srok* is appointed every three years by the *Achnha Luong* who reviews the lists of the registered population.

# 10 - PHNEAK NGEAR

Besides the *Kromokar*, in the provinces there exist other civil servants called *Phneak Ngear*, who bought from some mandarins of the crown the right to inflict sentences for certain specific offences. The complete account of these attributions, closely linked to Cambodian legislation, would take us too far, and in fact it will be included in a study on the Code which we will publish later.

Let us limit ourselves here and say that the titles, the assignments of the *Phneak Ngear*, vary a lot, as well as their number for each province. Let us list, for example, those who exist in one or two provinces.

In *Bati*, the *Chaufai* who has the title *Oknha Vongsa Anchut Aahk* with tent *pahn*, the *Pheak Ngear* are :

1 - The *Menou Reachea Sangkreem* who, from the *Joumreech*, bought the right to prosecute for thefts, murders, quarrels, brawls, and also one part of the sentences inflicted for those crimes or offences.

2 - The *Muntrey Anchut*, from the *Maha Muntrey* bought the right to watch over the inheritances of the mandarins who die leaving no next of kin. If these mandarins leave behind women, their inheritance, called *meardak*, is divided into three parts: one for the women, one for pious work and one for the king. It is divided into two parts if there are not any women.

3 - The *Reachea Thuppedey*,

4 - The *Muntrey Sena*, and

5 - The *Pipheak Vongsa* respectively get their responsibilities from the *Sauphea Thuppedey*, the *Muntrey Kotdarach* and from the *Pipheak Vinichey*. And one of the main assignments of these three persons consists in condemning the women of the province who would marry another man before burning the remains of the deceased one.

6 - The *Chau Ponhea Norea Sena* obtained from the *Jouthea Sangkreem Thuppedey* the right, for a fee, to deliver a second letter of release to hereditary slaves (*pol* or *neak ngear*) who manage to redeem themselves. The first one was delivered by their own chiefs.

7 - The *Vongsa Tup Reech* obtained from the *Pipheak Tup Reachea Chang Veang* the right to affix his stamp on the letter which the previous *vongsa* delivered, again for a fee. The redeemed slave must not ignore that in case of negligence a sentence would await him and later on if he did not have any money, a slavery of a new kind.

8 - The *Pipheak Vongsa*, from the *Vongsa Thuppedey*, bought the right to sell the ordinary men (*reas*) who were exempt from the tax lists.

9 - The *Menou Mohengsa* gets from the *Pohuletep* the right to sell the buffaloes' thieves. The retrieved buffaloes must be handed over to him.

Cambodian prisoners, 1866-1875, KMV

10 - The *Muntrey Sneha,* and

11 - the *Menou Rota*, respectively get from the *Rot Sena* and from the *Luong Pipheak*, the right to punish the bull thieves and that of laying their hand on the lost bulls.

12 - The *Menou Banha Auphea* received from the *Oknha Thomsena Thuppedey* the right to sentence those who are guilty of incest, or marrying a woman within their close family.

13 - The *Menou Kuchen* gets from the *Oknha Anten* the right of receiving 12 *damlang* from the product of the sentences inflict-

ed by the *Menou* (no. 1), he also receives seven *damlang* for each sentence inflicted on men and women who flee together.

14 - Finally, the *Essoren Muntrey Chang Vang* whose assignments consist in receiving the part which goes to the king for each sentence, has the *Chomnit Essoreahk* as a delegate to receive that particular part in the province of *Bati*.

As a rule, in all the judiciary sentencing, three parts should be as follows: one for the king, one for the governor, one for the competent *Phneak Ngear*. The cases which are not within the *Phneak Ngear*'s assignments are judged by the governor or his *krom*okar.

In the province of *Saang*, far less important but being more or less equal in area and population to one of our ordinary cantons in Cochinchina, we find:

1 - the *Phneak Ngear* of the *Joumreech*, who is the *Menou*: thefts, murders, disputes.

2 - The *Reachea Thuppedey* (*sedam*).

3 - The *Sena Thuppedey* (*chhveng*) who bought from the *Sauphea Thuppedey* the right to sentence the adulteresses and the pregnant single young ladies.

4 - The *Pohuletep* has the *Menou Mohengsa*: buffaloes.

5 - The *Prea Sdach* has the *Menou Banha*: insulting one's elders, one's parents, one's uncles or aunts, marrying a woman near the pagoda where one was a member of a religious order.

6 - The *Pibol* who has the right to fish on the 'posterior' river [the western or Bassac River], sells the titles of *Menou Neavi* of *Phea Kedey Neavi* to two persons, with the right of ownership of small fishing boats found on the banks of the province of Saang.

We will not talk about the Cambodian law in this note. Let us only say that in the Khmer language, sentencing means selling (*lok*); and in actual fact, all cases end up in a sale, with the freeing of the convicted person as a forfeit if he does not redeem himself by paying the amount of the sentencing.

## 11 - CASTES

Neither the mandarins, appointed and revoked depending on the whim of the king, nor the monks, who take a vow of chastity and the majority of whom only stay in their religious order for a very limited period of time, cannot be regarded as hereditary castes. Neither do we recognize the slaves, although they pass their condition onto their children, because, in principle, they can always redeem themselves, and because, in reality, redeeming oneself is common. But, in Cambodia, there exist two hereditary castes, pale reflections, what's more, of those whose civil and religious law sanctions the privileges so rigorously in the Brahmanic India. They are the *Bakou* and the *Prea Vongsa*.

The *Bakou* descend from the cast of the Brahmanes (*Puoch Preem*). In Siam they have brothers whose condition we ignore and with whom they have some connection. In Bangkok, they have a Brahmanic temple (*Baut Preem*) where the current chief of the Cambodian *Bakou* studied during his youth. The *Bakou* identity is passed on via the males. As a matter of fact the marriages outside the cast are rare although not forbidden by law. The Cambodians believe they are disastrous (*changray*), mostly those of *Bakou* girls with Khmer men.

The *Bakou* dress like other Cambodians, from whom they physically distinguish themselves by their hair, which they wear long and coiled up, the Annamese way.

They are Buddhist and some become monks when they are very young, and so they shave their head according to the rule. Their women are exactly the same as other Cambodian women. The *Bakou*'s daily activities are the same as the other Khmer. Spread all over the kingdom, they are not exempt from tax anymore as in the past. They have special chiefs chosen by the king from within their caste; there are seven of them. The highest-ranked bears the title *Prea Esey Phahs*; the others are the *Prea Tep Acha, the Prea Thamreech*, the *Prea Bamicha*, the *Prea En* (Indra), the *Prea Prohm* (Brahma), the *Prea Reem* (Rama).

The *Bakou* play a big role in all the royal ceremonies. They recite special phrases (*akum*), incomprehensible to the Cambodians and probably written in sanskrit.

This caste has a specific function: the care of the sacred sword (*Prea Khan*).

The *Bakou* are summoned in turn from all around the kingdom, in groups of ten or twelve, to serve for a month near the ancient broad sword in a special wing of a building at the palace.

Twice a week, on Tuesdays and Saturdays, at around seven o'clock in the morning, after the reciting of ritual phrases, some person draws the venerated relic out of its sheath and displays it on a carpet in the room where it is usually kept. A European is allowed to see it then, but only if the *Bakou* are ensured that they have been given the authorization by the king. It is a weapon made of steel, wide and short, on which are represented the main brahmanic divinities. The old sheath, which one believes was lost, has been replaced by another one, relatively modern, richly gilded and lacquered. This sheath is wrapped in red velvet and placed in a case.

As Janneau explains: "It is thanks to the *Bakou*'s care that the precious sword, which was hidden several times without doubt during the critical periods of interior troubles and invasions, has been kept intact and arrived to us passing through all kinds of disruptions which Cambodia has so often suffered."

There are between eight hundred and one thousand *Bakou* men. According to a well spread opinion in Cambodia, if the current royal family (*prea* vong) happened to die out, it is within the *Bakou* cast that the Khmers should choose a new one, among all those whom, as much as possible, have remained pure of marriages outside their caste.

It is under the name *Prea* or *Prea Vongsa* (divine lineage) that one calls the descendants, male or female, of the royal family, who having for several generations lost all contact with the kings and princes allied to the other Cambodians, are not regarded as having any right whatsoever to the throne.

Just like the *Bakou*, they are rather numerous, spread all around the kingdom and are not exempted from taxes anymore as they used to be in the past. One presumes that they enjoyed a lot of privileges, but now they are less esteemed than the *Bakou*, who have succeeded in keeping the purity of their race. The only advantage that they have is to be called *prea* in the acts or official lists, instead of *Chau*, a name used for the other Cambodians and which could be compared with our 'Sir'.

Belonging to the race of the *Prea Vongsa* is the family of the *Sdach Meahk*, an honorary mandarin with ten *pahn*, who, every year and for three days, was the king of the festivities of *Meahk* (see 'Festivities' further down).

A rustic Cambodian house, 1866-1875, KMV

## 12 - WATER OF THE OATH

The ceremony which consists in drinking the water of the oath (*phak tuk sebat*) takes place twice a year in the months of *Chet* and *Phatrabot*, in a pagoda of the capital, usually that of *Louk sang Kreech*.

For that occasion large new jars filled with water are set up and near them, monks recite prayers for three days. On the fixed day, all the mandarins from the interior of all the *samrap*, all the governors, the mandarins of the exterior, as well as those who are not in functions anymore, must go to that pagoda where the royal weapons are being carried by pages assigned to their care (*Kromoseng*).

The *Bakou* call upon the spirits, say unintelligible phrases which are proper to them, while stirring the water, which has been prepared and blessed, with the royal weapons. The mandarins enter the pagoda to drink the water: first the *Khnang Pos*, then the *Chado Sedam*, the *Sdach Tranh*, the mandarins with nine, eight, etc... *pahn*, without distinction of *samrap*. In small groups of three, four, five, they listen to an *alahk* reciting the phrase of the oath (*Satra Pram Theem*). They repeat its words as the reading proceeds, and from the hands of the *Bakou* receive the water in small cups made of bronze (*samriet*), a metal to which the Cambodians grant the virtue of giving a virtual force to pronounced words, something which prevents one from worrying about the mental restrictions, the insincerity of the person who swears.

After the ceremony, the list of all the mandarins present is drawn and handed to the *Ruon Luong* who are, for the *Samrap* Ek, the *Maha Tep* and the *Maha Muntrey*, for the *Samrap Tou*, the *Thireech Vongsa* commonly called *Reech Ansa*, and for the *Samrap Trey* and the *Thireech Muntrey*.

If a mandarin fails, the *Ruon Luong* have to make him carry the water and require from him as many *damlang*, that is to say as many times sixteen 'ligatures' as his dignity contains *pahn* [thousand].

This fine is shared between the *Ruon Luong* and the suzerain (*Chaufai Kamnan*) of the penalised mandarin.

If a sick mandarin informs them on time, the water is brought to his home and he does not have to pay anything.

While the mandarins are drinking at the pagoda, at the palace the *obbaioureech*, the *obbarach* and all the princes, members of the royal family drink in the throne room. The ceremony takes place exactly like outside the palace. The water is brought from the pagoda.

We know that several wings of buildings are practically divided into two parts by a wall which, over the whole length of the palace, separates the reception part from the private part. The throne room, therefore, has an interior part where the king grants his women an audience. In this private room, first the *Prea Voreechini* and all the princesses drink, then all the *Prea Meneang, Prea Meang,* and the *Saulek* who gather in groups of four or five for one *alahk*. Without doubt, for a majority of these women, the oath of faithfulness here has a double significance, a political and conjugal one.

On the occasion of these ceremonies, the governors give the king traditional presents through the *Maha Tep* and the *Maha Muntrey*. Those gifts are proportional to the number of *sahk*. For example, a mandarin with seven *pahn* will offer 70 *krechas* of rice (the *krechas* is a measure weighing 4 Cambodian pounds), 70 pounds of *ko* cotton (*gon*, in Annamese), 70 pounds of *koka* cotton (another species, a big tree with pretty red flowers); 70 pounds of safran (*romiet*); 70 pounds of yellow 'Campeche wood' (*khnor*, jackfruit tree, or *kle*, yet another

Campeche wood); 70 pounds of nettles from China (*khechey*); 7 pounds of almonds from *Thelok* to make some oil, 3 pounds and a half of vegetable wax (*kremnon chambak*), and various other presents such as hens, ducks, etc...

A governor with ten *pahn* will give 100 *krechas* of rice, etc., 5 pounds of vegetable wax.

Most of those presents are given only once a year, usually in *Chet*. And so, the mandarins who have carried out this obligation only bring the rice, the ducks, the hens in *Phatrabot*.

The governors still give the king traditional presents of rice during the festivities of *Kadak* and *Meahk* (see the section 'Festivals' further down).

The Royal Palace in Phnom Penh, ca 1870, MAE

## 13 - REVENUES

The revenues of the kingdom of Cambodia, at the moment, amount to three million francs. They can be classified into four categories in accordance with the collection mode.

The first and most important category comprises the big farms, awarded annually, revenues from Customs, opium, gambling, lottery and some fisheries. The Customs service takes a tenth, in kind or in cash, from all the imported merchandises.

The second category comprises various revenues from rural areas which are not leased and which the king has collected by small mandarins whom others supervise.

They are fields arable in cotton and mulberry trees, which are none other than the banks of the Big River and its islands, from the rapids all the way to *Banam*. The lots are measured in 'brasses', 6 feet (*phieem*); their depth is not fixed and depends on the nature of the terrain. Lots of 12 *brasses* are awarded for up to 60 'ligatures' per year. The lease is made in May and June by the small mandarins, the king's personal servants who pass on the lists to the *alahk*. The latter check these lists and collect the money, either immediately or after the harvest in March or April.

The brick houses which the king has had built in Phnom Penh come in lots or quarters of twenty units with a ground-floor and one storey. A unit is leased for between 12 and 15 piastres per month, depending on its location. The *alahk* responsible for the leasing are supervised by other members of staff of the palace.

The personal quoted value of Chinese and Annamese people varies from 10 to 30 'ligatures' a year. It is also collected by small mandarins from the palace, supervised by others, depending on the choice of the master.

The third category comprises certain taxes in nature demanded in some provinces, such as the iron of *Kampong* Soai, the cardamum and gamboge. The income is ensured by the governors of these provinces.

An so, in *Pursat*, the inhabitants wishing to pick cardamum declare it and bring 20 pounds (*neel*) of this seed every year. If they can't, due to a bad harvest, they have to deliver 40 pounds the following year.

In this category are likely to appear the presents which the governors give to the king (see 'Water of the Oath'), as well as the 10 cubits (*hat*) of cotton material that are woven by the families of ordinary men who are exempted from duties because of their disability.

In the fourth category, we will place the revenues which the king traditionally shares with some mandarins responsible for ensuring their collection. Most of these revenues (for example, several fisheries) are leased by a mandarin who, out of three units, keeps one and gives the king the other two.

In this category exist two taxes which are worth a special study, owing to the particularities they present: the tax on rice and the buying back of duties.

Phnom Penh buildings built and leased by the king,
1877, Private Collection

# 14 - TAX ON RICE

In the month of *Meahk Thom* (February) a royal delegate (*Achnha Luong*) and a delegate of storemen, two in number, leave Phnom Penh to visit each province. The two men divide the kingdom, the *Pohuletep* (*sedam*) for one, the *Phipheak Salev* (*chhveng*) for the other. Their own delegate, called the *Mehang*, and the *Achuha Luong*, carrying the royal order (*prea bantul*), visit the governor of the province who gives them an extra delegate (*bamro*) and, the three of them, go round to all the villages of that province.

In every village, the inhabitants have built a shelter (*roung*) in advance near which they have placed a small bamboo trestle on which the delegates will be able to wash (*reeng ngut tuk*). Upon their arrival they read out the royal order to the *me srok* who pledges to take them to all the houses and not to conceal anything. Traditionally, he has to pay them a 'ligature' for the reading[1].

In the past, paying for the reading out of the royal order was optional for ordinary men. They would negotiate the price with the delegates to whom they also gave a piece of cloth. In doing this they were buying back the setting of the tax which was not applied in their province. This practice does not exist anymore.

The *me srok* pays the cost of the pledge (*thlay sebat*) fixed at one 'ligature' of 'sapeque', at one five cubit piece of cotton, at four *chom* which are bits of banana tree trunks in which a few arek nuts and betel leaves have been placed. According to an old custom, one of the delegates, after bathing on the trestle, wraps himself up with that piece of cotton.

---

1 This year, four, five and even up to twelve 'ligatures' 'were demanded of certain *me srok* from the province of *Ba Phnom*, which we were passing through at that time. They intended to complain to the grand mandarins of the crown (*As Chumnum*) in Phnom Penh).

A Cambodian village next to the river, 1866-1875, KMV

In a Cambodian village, 1866-1875, KMV

The shelter (*roung*) built for the three delegates belongs to the *Achnha Luong* who can request its transportation to his home in Phnom Penh. Therefore, the *me srok,* who would be well advised to buy back this small quantity of straw huts and bamboo, discusses it before the departure of the *Achnha Luong.* The price varies between three and ten '*ligatures.*'

Of course, the *me srok* will take the oath where there is a fearful spirit (*neak ta, areak puke*). Finally, all these preliminaries being accomplished, he takes the three delegates to evaluate the harvest and determine the percentage which each inhabitant must take to the royal stores.

And so out of ten *thang* (*gia*, in Annamese) of harvest, the king levies one *thang*.

Moreover, for one *thang* which the king gets, one must give:

1 - One *tau* (1/2 *thang* of paddy for the chiefs of the *Bakou* (*Srau Bakou*).

2 - One *khsok* (measure costing three or four Cambodian pounds) of paddy for food (a unit) for the rats (*srau bai kandor*)

3 - One *khsok* of rice called 'walking rice' (*ângkâr choeûng pon*).

4 - One pound of rice (*neel*) called 'Opening of Stores' Door (*angkar Bok Thvea*r).

5 - One pound for the deletion on the catalogues (name of the tax payer, after paying his tax), (*Angkar Lup Banhchi*).

6 - Five wreaths of palm leaves (*slak tenet*) or straw (*sebau*) to cover the stores.

7 - Five battens of bamboo (*chamrahk rusey*) for the store's trellis (*roneep*).

8 - Five rattan sticks (*dom phdau*) to use as bonds.

9 - One hen, four eggs, and a bottle of rice spirits.

All these articles, except for the paddy of the *Bakou*, are for the storemen who usually demand only rice in kind (see no. 2, 3, 4, and 5); the price of the other articles is discussed between the *Mehang* and the inhabitants.

The share of the chiefs of the *Bakou* varies from half a *tau* to one *thang*; they do not get anything if the king gets less than half a *thang*; if he gets more than two *thang*, their share remains fixed at one *thang*.

10 - Moreover, all inhabitants who pay the king less than two *thang*, that is to say who have less than twenty *thang* in store, have to give the delegates three bowls (*tok*) of rice, each containing three pounds (*neel*). Those who pay more than two *thang* are exempted from this.

So, one can see that a poor inhabitant, whose harvest is, for example, worth five *thang*, that is to say about two *pikuls* of 60 kilos, pays a heavy tax: one *tau* to the king, half a *tau* to the *Bakou*, and all the articles that follow, down to and including the *Angkar Chumnum*; if the inhabitant has ten *thang*, his tax is slightly smaller; only the share of the king and that of the *Bakou* amount proportionally to his asset. And if he has more than twenty *thang*, he does not pay the *Angkar Chumnum* anymore, only the share of the king matches the proportion of the tenth, the other articles remain fixed.

Their visit done, the three delegates then inform the governor about the result. The latter is entitled to the tenth of the king's share. One can presume that, in most provinces, he has a source of products from the mission of his delegate: the latter having his share of rice from the people, he gets some 'ligatures' and pieces of cotton which are the price of the oath.

The tenth of the governor's share being deducted, the nine remaining tenths go to the capital. Here too another tenth of the share is deducted for the storemen. They, in their turn and for a few years now, have to give the *Louk Veang* a tenth of their share.

The transportation to Phnom Penh is entirely the tax payers' responsibility, a heavy cost for a lot of the provinces. One praises men whose job it is to transport and who, very well known and for good reasons, enjoy the trust of the public. This is not indifferent; if these men ran away, if the rice, at the time, was not delivered, it would be highly inconvenient for the responsible tax payer. To these porters, the inhabitants of the provinces which are far away from the capital give a quantity of rice, as salary, equal to that they must take to Phnom Penh.

A considerable part of the harvest is exported during the few months between the beginning of the harvest and the time fixed for the tour of the the *Mehang*. The *Louk Veang* leases customs posts prior to the collection of the tenth on the rice exempted from the fixed tax. The farmer of each province establishes customs posts, as he pleases, until the day the round of the delegates is over.

The governor employs an agent who, for the record, takes into account the income of this farmer. The province of *Ba Phnom*, which, together with that of *Pursat*, is the most productive in rice, is given for these three month long customs duties, depending on the year, two or three thousand *thang*, payable in kind or cash depending on the stipulation of the *Veang*. The latter gets one share out of three of the profit of these customs posts, the other two go to the king.

The *Bakou* and the *Prea Vong*, exempted in the past, now pay the tax on rice. The very rare exemptions provided by the *Veang* are presented to the three delegates by those who hold them, and whose names are registered for the record.

With this brief outline of the organisation of Cambodia, one can imagine the extent and the importance of the current *Veang*'s powers, particularly seconded by the *Alara Chenda*, chief of the royal secretaries.

All these attributions are not inherent in the *Veang*'s dignity, and for sure the current official would keep most of them should he become *Chaufea*, a high position which seems to be reserved for him. Demanding and tight-fisted with the State's money, talented with a great understanding of the multiple details of his administration, this precious humble servant of the king of Cambodia in himself and at the highest degree sums up the qualities of order, regularity and calculated slowness which, under his impulsion, his subordinates bring in their financial accountancy. The lack of popularity which is attached to any good treasurer having to control the collecting of onerous taxes, is not lacking in him moreover, and has, it seems, already once caught the king's wish to confer on him the title of *Chaufea*.

A rich man's home, 1866-1875, KMV

# 15 - KAMLANG. - BUYING BACK OF DUTIES

In accordance with a very old custom, all the men in the population were divided up in forces (*kamlang*) of the grand and small mandarins. They would choose as chief (*chaufai, neey kamlang*) any mandarin whichever they pleased. And in the *kamlang* of a grand mandarin were included, on top of the men who had chosen him personally, all the *kamlang* of the inferior mandarins, his subordinates. So that the various *kamlang* merged in four big *kamlang*, the chiefs of which (*chaufai*) were the *Chado Sedam*. These four *kamlang* together formed only one which recognised the *Chaufea* as their chief. This first minister, moreover, had his personal *kamlang*, composed of the men who had chosen him and of *kamlang* of the mandarins under his order, such as the *alahk*.

The mandarins *Suos Dey*, responsible for the registers of the population and the duties, asked the big chiefs (*chaufai*) for men. The chiefs ordered the subordinate chiefs (*neey*) to choose men depending on the importance of their respective *kamlang*. The duties sometimes lasted for three months a year.

Often the ordinary men (*reas*) brought their *neey kamlang* some presents such as rice, hens, ducks. The *neey kamlang* kept one share for himself and gave the other two to the *chaufai*. Many men, thanks to these presents, avoided the corvees. The governors, whose job finally was to ensure the levying of the men of the province, in that operation saw a source of guaranteed income, since the people liable to corvee, as much as possible, were trying to buy it back.

For six years now, some considerable modifications were introduced to this institution. The *kamlang* remains, but it is personal, or at the most reaches the lower chiefs. And so the various *kamlang* of the *alahk* enter that of the *Alara Chenda*, their chief, but do not mix anymore with that of the *Oknha Veang*, the head chief. The grand mandarins have only their personal *kamlang*.

Every three years, the registers of the able and strong people are checked. From Phnom Penh, a royal delegate (*Achnha Luong*), leaves, accompanied by a delegate of the mandarins responsible for the registers (*bamro' Suos Dey*) together with a delegate of the suzerain of the province (*bamro' chaufai kamnan khet*). These three individuals go to the governor of the province who, after reading the royal order (*prea bantul*), assigns one of his subordinates (*kromokar*), who knows the province well, to accompany them.

In every village, the royal order is read to the *me srok* who pays its cost, fixed at one *bat* (a Cambodian silver coin with a value of four 'ligatures'), one piece of cotton measuring five cubits, and two candles. Then the *me srok* takes the oath not to conceal anything, to sincerely abide by the word of the master of lives. All the men of the village are summoned to the place where the royal messenger's shelter has been built. Their name, age and condition are written down: free, slave or *neak ngear*; as well as those of the mandarin, the person of their choice for chief of the *kamlang*. Those aged between fifteen and eighteen and those above fifty are registered for the record; also if they are disabled. The well and strong men between eighteen and fifty are the men liable to corvee who today buy back their corvee for twenty 'ligatures' 'of sapeque, plus two 'ligatures' for the waste; in silver, ten Mexican piastres for three men, or one bar (*nen*) for five. The mandarins' slaves, in general, do not have to pay. Those of the ordinary men are taxed ten 'ligatures' which their master pay for them; they are registered in the same *kamlang* as him.

The hereditary royal slaves (*pol, neak ngear*) can only choose as chief of *kamlang* their own chiefs (*chaufai*). The free men (*neak chea*) may choose among all the mandarins, big or small, of the kingdom.

A copy of the list of the registered population of the village is left with the *me srok*. Once the three delegates have covered the entire province, they return to Phnom Penh where the governor asks for the copy of the lists of his province. The registers of the whole kingdom are with the *Suos Dey,* from whom the mandarins can find out about their respective *kamlang*. They all have some, from the *Presor Saurivong,* who has about a thousand men, to the last *neey*, who have three, two, sometimes one, even only in his family.

Each chief is responsible for the paying of the tax of the men in his *kamlang*; he pays for them when one has fled or died during the three years between two updating. It is true that he is left with one share, generally the third, ten men out of thirty, for example; however, one supposes that this share varies depending on the personal position of this mandarin.

The money of the buying back of the corvees is not included in the financial accounts keeping of the *Oknha Veang*. Instead it is used to rent workers, buy pieces of equipment to raise buildings of all sorts.

However, the corvees are not totally bought back. Depending on the presumed needs of the royal court, every year two or three provinces are chosen and all their men liable to corvees have to go and work there or find a replacement. They cannot avoid their three-day corvee: the lists are by name and well kept. For the other provinces, there would be some improvement if the buying back was effective, but we have good reasons to believe that, generally, they have many chores to do after having paid the twenty 'ligatures.'

A Cambodian Buddhist monk, 1866-1875, MAE

# 16 - RELIGION

The religion of the Khmers is the southern Buddhism or the Ceylon Buddhism, a set of principles about which so many publications of merit have been issued that here we will simply give the meaning of some of the main religious terms used by the Cambodians, and express some reflections which are suggested by this tolerant religion which spread only through predication and persuasion. It has a huge impact on all the people of Indochina whose home country is Ceylon and who have best retained the purity of the teaching of the master whom the Cambodians call *Prea Put* or simply *Prea* (divine, sacred), and whom they distinguish from the other Buddha by the name *Samonokoudam* (*Cramana Gaoutama*, the ascetic of the *Gotamides*).

The location of eternal felicity is *Nirpeen* (Nirvana). The triple gem is the *Trey Rot* (*Triratna*) composed of Buddha, *Putthea;* law, *Thommea* (Dharma); and the congregation of the Clergy, *Sangkhea*. The Triple Basket is the *Prea Trey Beydak* (*Tripitaka*), the three parts of which are Discourse, *Prea* Saut (*Soutra*); Discipline, *Prea Viney* (*Vinaya*); and Metaphysics, *Prea Apithom* (*Abhidharma*). The mountain in the centre of the four buddhist worlds (*thvep* or *loukey*, world, island) is the *Prea Some*, which has in the east the *Boviti Thvip* (*Vidcha*), in the north the *Udar Koro Thvip* (*Kourou*), in the west the *Amarokouiani Thvip* (Godani), in the south the *Chumpou Thvip* (*Djambou*), the latter being the world inhabited by our planet.

The great ascetics, the hermits, are the *Maha Rosey* or *Eysey* (*Maha rischis*).

The Buddhist monks or *talapoins* (a 16th Century French word for a Buddhist monk) called *Louk Sang, Meak Buos, Neak Joeung, Phikou* (*Bhikshous*, beggar) live in monasteries (*Wat Kedey*). They wear yellow robes, shave their heads, live on charity and eat one meal a day only, sometimes two, before mid-day. They teach the children reading and writing. These children, before the age of twelve, are called *sek* (parrots). From this young age they can go into holy orders and observe certain prescriptions, so that, say the Cambodians, through the merits that they acquire, they pay the debt of gratitude which they owe their mother. They are then called *nen* or *samne*. At the age of 21, in order to pay the same type of debt towards their father, they join the holy orders for a period of time which varies between a few days and their whole life.

One must admit that the Buddhist monasticism is facilitated by the miserable social and political state of all these regions; in the middle of troubles and disorders, these religious people have a relative tranquility. And, it seems to us that, in our possessions, their number tends to be reduced, the population enjoying a more considerable security and well-being.

In our province of *Tra Vinh*, free of all secular influence, the monks, gathered in a general meeting, elect a head called *Louk Opechhea*. He supervises the conduct of all the monks, gives them the authorisation to leave the orders, and expels the unworthy ones. Underneath him, also elected for an undetermined time, are the *Louh Aup*, whose number is not specified. They give the authorisation to join a religious order and take to the *Opechhea* the monks who request to leave. The *Louk Kru Saut*, monks who have the reputation of being educated, have more or less the same functions. They are appointed by the *opechhea* together with the chiefs of pagoda called *Louk Sangkreech* or *Me Vaht*.

In Cambodia, two high dignitaries, the *Louk Sang Lrech* or *Louk Sdach* and the *Prea Socon*, chosen by the king, are most honored but have a rather limited authority. In the end, their only authority is the teaching of Buddha whose ideas are contrary to that of the institutions of this type which were tried out more or less successfully in the various countries where the Ceylon Buddhism has been adopted.

The Cambodians' fervent piety makes them respect and

greatly worship their monks; provided, however, that the latter observe their rules the main precepts of which everybody knows. The respects are for the sacred character of the monk who wears the yellow robe and not at all for the person. The secular power, although showing some consideration, can use their rules against them, should the monks try to intervene in politics. Let us add here that for a long time now the Cambodians have always been exemplary in this respect. We have never heard that the monks of our possessions had the slightest conflict with our authorities.

The care with which they observe their vow of chastity is quite remarkable, too. The Cambodian law, it is true, adds the punishment of the secular arm to the anathema of the Master, but in our provinces where this support does not exist, the monks' behaviour, all the same, is impeccable. Maybe justice is administered without our magistrates being aware of it, and a Cambodian person would never denounce facts of that kind to them. The best attitude, in actual fact, would be to seem to ignore them up to a certain point.

Despite the absurdity of the dogmas of their doctrine, it is difficult to refrain from feeling some respect inspired by the kindness and selflessness of these religious men. But, solely and selfishly occupied by their salvation, they do not regard themselves as being responsible for other souls; that is the cause of the main qualities of this clergy as well as its imperfections.

Apart from this strong religion, virtually official, one must take into account the belief in all the divinities of Brahmanism, a belief which Buddhism allowed to subsist by altering it. Above all, one must take into account a cult which merges with this belief, the worship of genies and ancestors (*areak, mimout, neak ta*) which as altars has forests, mountains, above all ruins, the remains of which, in the eyes of the Khmers, manifests the power of these genies, and where we others recognise a civilisation, the veil of which is to be lifted.

The oath, very much used in administration, as we saw, is also frequently used in justice. To take the oath, the Cambodians repeat, word after word, a formula pronounced by a well read person, the *Sacha Pranitheen*, or more commonly known as the *Satra Pramtheen*. It is a long enumeration of all the spirits dreaded in Cambodia who are referred to by the name of their residence. The person who takes the oath invokes their aid, if he is sincere, but demands their punishment if he fails to keep his word.

Buddhist monks at Angkor Wat, 1866, MAE

# 17 - SLAVERY

Apart from free men (*neak chea, prey ngear*), in Cambodia there are three clear categories of slaves:

1 - The servants, *khhnom*, slaves because of debts, who in principle have the imprescriptible right to redeem themselves by wiping out their debt, or to change master every time they find a new one who accepts to pay off the previous one. Sometimes they are not attached to a personal service and may have a profession, with the agreement of the master who takes an important share of the profits, letting them have hardly the hope of earning enough to redeem themselves. The possibility of buying oneself back is less and less possible if slavery persists and if the master increases the debt by the amount of the value of the clothes, for example, which which he provides his slave. Slavery is supposed to only make up for the interests of the debt but does not wipe out the capital. Slavery, generally, is not too harsh, thanks to the lazy apathy of the masters, and so this curse is less serious in itself than because of the abuses and demoralisation which it drags with it. It is closely linked to the big plague of Cambodia, its administration of justice. Most of the slaves are there because of a condemnation or a judiciary sale (*lok*).

2 - The savages, *Penong* or *Stieng*, whose trade is done by the Laotians who direct them towards *Sambok*. These poor people, missing their forests and their freedom, die mainly at the beginning of their stay in Cambodia. Once they are used to their condition, they are more reliable and helpful than the Cambodians.

3 - The hereditary royal slaves (*pol* or *neak ngear*) are relatives of descendants of great criminals and rebels. Either these condemned persons had their death penalty commuted with confiscation of them and their descendants, or after their death, by aggravation, their family was reduced to this condition. Others come from prisoners of war, for example, representing a small colony of Laotians in *Peem Sedey*, north of the border of our provinces of *Tanan* and *Chaudoc*.

A "savage" Moi dressed for war, 1866-1875, MAE

The largest part is at the service of the king. Several serve big mandarins to whom they have been handed over by the king. Others are assigned to the maintenance of certain pagodas.

All the *neak ngear* of the kingdom are registered by name, on special lists. They owe their master three or four months of service per year. The rest of the year, they reside where they want and use their time as they please. They can prosper, acquire a certain affluence, and yet not find it easier to redeem themselves, their chiefs (*chaufai*) then becoming more demanding. A master has no right over the slaves' properties; he can only have their person, or a replacement, at their service for the fixed period of time, but then their work is very hard, one feels a bit sorry for them; the satellites of a master are all the more pitiless in that the *neak ngear* has the reputation of not being totally reduced to complete poverty.

The slaves' wives have to weave pieces of cotton for the master; the latter must provide the material which is seldom sufficient for the task.

A Cambodian minister surrounded by his servants,
1866-1875, MAE

Sometimes the *neak ngear* enter into an alliance with free families; the children, as soon as they reach the age at which they are under orders, are then split up in the following manner: the first child, the third, etc... follow the condition of their father; the second and fourth child, that of the mother. If there is an even number of children, the value of the youngest is estimated by a *chaufai pol*, one part is attributed to the father and two to the mother, and the child is bought back by paying the third or two thirds of the estimation, depending on whether the father or the mother is the slave. The same is true for an only child. Children from mixed marriages, and whose fate has not yet been decided, bear the special name of *pah*n*h kot*.

Cambodian musicians, 1866-1870, MAE

## 18 - HABITS AND CUSTOMS

Very apathetic and lethargic, the Cambodians are less deceitful than the Annamese although they try. They are less hospitable. On the main roads, various inns called *sala*, or *tram* or again precham chun, provide a shelter to the travellers. Elsewhere the latter must present themselves to the *me srok* who will find some accommodation for them. If the inhabitants are informed in advance of the arrival of a mandarin, they will build a temporary shelter for him. But the head of a hut, the Cambodian, generally does not view the arrival of a guest with great pleasure.

The sons of those who live comfortably are brought up at the pagoda as soon as they reach the age of six to eight (see the chapter on Religion). A young girl brought up at home leads a very secluded life when she reaches the age of consent, hence the strange expression of 'a young girl who goes into obscurity' (*kremom chaul molop*). Thanks to numerous moral precepts inculcated quite early by a mother in her daughter, perhaps also thanks to strict laws, the habits of the Cambodian women, above all disregarding the capital city, are far less dissolute than those of the women in neighboring countries.

The Khmer people love music and poetry. Their chants, accompanied by instruments playing simple and charming melodies, although a little monotonous, are often dialogues improvised by a man and a woman giving each other their amorous cues, and the clever interpreters in this type of exercise are highly regarded. Obsessions, pleas from the lover, more or less prolonged and resisting pretence from the young girl, and finally confession of a shared mutual love, such is obviously the program. Images inspired by the moon, the stars, the breeze, the flowers, the trees, even by the thunder embellish that recurrent but never outdated theme, with which for six thousand years in all countries a young man has been entertaining a young girl.

The national garment is the *langouti* (*sampot*), common to both sexes, in the same way as in Siam and Laos. The men's outfit is a narrow tunic buttoning up at the front, in the middle, with numerous buttons. The women wear a narrow sheath dress slightly flared at the collar. In Phnom Penh, less loyal to the outfit than to the *langouti*, men and women wrap themselves in a colorful scarf leaving their arms bare. Sometimes in order to look smart, the men wear a waistcoat with short sleeves, called a 'european outfit' (*au bareang*).

Moreover and for important events, they have the 'dress for ceremonies' called *au phai*.

A Cambodian woman, 1866-1875, MAE

For their hair, the Siamese customs have been adopted at the royal court. The shaving of the topknot takes place at the age of 11 to 13 for the girls and before 15 for the boys. The men, the women and the girls shave their heads, letting their hair grow two or three centimetres on the top. As is the old Cambodian custom, still generally observed in the provinces, the men and the women who are married have to wear their hair short, but not shaved off. The young girls' hair must cover their nape, in the Ninon style, which is a much more elegant fashion. Where the two races are mixed, they often wear their hair long just like the Annamese women, but plaiting it in a slightly different way.

The food is similar to that of the Annamese, but inferior in terms of preparation. For the ingredients, the Cambodians use a lot of unripe fruit. Those who eat with chopsticks instead of with their fingers are quite rare, contrary to their neighbors, the Cochinchinese.

A Cambodian dwelling, 1866-1875, MAE

Their houses erected on stilts are built according to fixed rules from the old treaties (*Kebuon*); they rarely depart from them. They are composed of three compartments (*loveng*). A high pointed roof, covers the private living space called *Kro*. Four trusses support this roof, which on one, two or three sides is extended but with a gentle slope in order to cover a space used for the domestic functions and the bamboo trellis of which, being the floor, is slightly lower than that of the actual habitation. This lower part of their house is called *chhnieng*.

## Marriages

If polygamy, beneficial to the current social state, is practiced by the important and rich people, it is however contrary to the instinct of this people whose women are proud, jealous and vindictive. In actual fact, the first wife (*propon dom*) enjoys much more authority and consideration. Ceremonies exist just for her which vary somewhat depending on the villages, but which we present here as a whole.

A woman who, in this case is nicknamed *Chechau*, is sent by the parents of the boy to sound out the young girl's parents and see if a proposal will be honored. Ensured of the consent, they ask some messengers, men and women, to make the official proposal (*dandeng*). These messengers are the *neak phlau* (the guides). They carry presents called *sla kamchahp peak* (areca to ease the talking, to conclude). These presents consist of one hundred areca nuts, two hundred betel leaves, one pound of gambier, a flask of wine, one pound of tobacco. Part of these presents is the house which will be the young couple's home, near that of the young girl's parents; the fiancé has to see to its construction before the wedding.

Upon the arrival of the *neak phlau*, the fiancée's father and mother summon their relatives, their neighbors and announce: "Here are the *neak phlau* who have come to propose to our daughter". The presents are consumed by all the guests, then an envoy speaks up and says: "All of you have accepted our presents; therefore, this young girl becomes the wife of the person sending us them, as from now he will come and serve you, you the fiancée's parents; do not be harsh on him". Then a big meal is served, after which the marriage is regarded as concluded. From that moment, if the young girl takes another husband, is unfaithful to her fiancé, the latter has the rights which the law grants the husband.

Before leaving, the *neak phlau* ask the fiancée's parents to stipulate the arrangements for the banquet (*bangkahp pe rebas rihpkar*). If the boy's family wishes to bear the expense, generally they comply with the old custom which consists in providing five 'pikuls' of pork meat, that is to say about three hundred kilos, fifty hens, thirty ducks, one hundred bottles of rice wine and thirty cakes called *phle ahhoeu* (fruit).

The celebration then follows but the day can vary, it can be after one day or several years. When the moment approaches, the young man's family sends for an expert in the knowledge of lucky or unlucky days, and asks him to choose a favorable day; and they send a *neak phlau* to suggest (*chun*) that day to the other family. The latter indicates a location proper to the building of the shelter under which the banquet will take place, and the day before the chosen day the fiancé's parents take him there.

In the evening, monks come and recite prayers. The fiancée wraps a kind of turban (*rebai*) around her head. The young man dresses up and the two of them squat next to each other and listen to the prayers. Then a man on the fiancé's side, called *neak maha*, asks the young girl's parents: "For your daughter, how much *Kansla* money is needed?" The reply: "Our daughter costs money, usually 19 *damlang*, 10 *slang*."[1]

That same night, in some venues, an original ceremony takes place, the Cambodians call it *bihm thyoeu thmenh* (chew to cut one's teeth). It is done in two different ways: the Laotian and the Cambodian way. For the Laotian chewing mode (*bihm lev*) one takes a bit of varnish called *ampul leahk*, which one

---

[1] This sum is estimated in a very old currency, called *prak takoung takong*, which is mentioned only in that occasion, at least to our knowledge. In this currency, one *damlang* is equivalent to 4 bat, 1 *bat* to 4 *slang*; and 6 *slang* are equivalent to one 'ligature' of sapeque in the current currency. The above mentioned sum of money, therefore, is equivalent to 52 'ligatures' and 6 *tiens*.

spreads on ginned cotton; the cotton is placed on a *tenot* leaf (flabellus borassus) and the whole lot is applied on the bride's teeth. The Cambodian chewing mode (*bihm khmer*) is carried out in the same way, but, in the morning, an expert (*acha*) puts a pick on the jar containing the ingredients, puts the jar on the fire to warm up the content and takes the exuding liquid to again coat the bride's teeth. The fire is supervised and maintained by four young girls.

The fiancée spends that last night in the new house. The fiancé sleeps under the shelter. Early in the morning, the latter puts on a ceremonial outfit (*au phai*), usually red colored, and goes up to his wife's parents. A young boy awaits him at the top of he ladder, guides him to a mat and receives one *damlang* in silver or in sapeques as salary. The groom bows down alone first; then some old women accompany the bride to his side, and the two of them bow down together.

A few arec flowers have been attached with cotton threads around three pieces of banana tree trunk. This is called the arec of the blessing (*sla prepo*). The young man offers one to his wife's father, another to her mother and the third to her brothers or other relative of hers. To this offering he adds: two torches, as big as the arm, called torches of salutation (*tien sampea*); one other pair of torches as big as a thumb, called *tien kamnaht*; the *kansla* money, that is to say a bar of silver plus five piastres. Let us add that the price of a mother's milk (*preak snap tuk do*) is one Cambodian piastre (*bat*). There is a considerable difference between the *kansla* sum traditionally requested, 52 'ligatures,' and that which is given today, which is equivalent to 135 'ligatures.'

While the married couple is still sitting on the mat, a male *neak phlau* ties their wrists up (*chang day*) with a cotton thread held by all the assistants while the parents, with torches in their hands, go around the couple seven times. Then the guests, depending on their wealth, give the newly weds presents, either silver items or sapeques [a French coin used in Indochina]. The husband follows his wife inside the house; she is taken there by the old women and he holds onto her by the end of her scarf. He then changes his clothes and they both go down to the shelter to supervise the banquet and take care of the guests. The groom serves his father-in-law, pours him some drink. In lower class people, often the father-in-law asks his new son-in-law to sing. Once the banquet is over, the guests, always in great numbers, leave, taking away with them some cakes. At nightfall the old women prepare the bedroom. The young man's mother joins her daughter-in-law there who, sitting next to her husband, takes a cake, called *nomier*, places a bit of it in his mouth, and in his turn, he does the same to his wife. With one hand the mother grasps her son's head and with the other her daughter-in-law's. She bangs the two heads against each other three times, saying: "Stay united, do not quarrel". The old women place a squash (*trelach*) into the bride's arms, saying: "May your union be as soft as this fruit, your children as numerous as grass leaves, and your grandchildren as numerous as rice balls. Be happy." Then they retire, leaving the newly-weds alone.

Three days later, the bride's whole family accompanies the couple to pay their respect to the groom's parents.

A son-in-law lives close to his wife's father and mother and helps them, serves them sometimes, either for a few years or even for life. According to the women, this custom is due to a victory, which once more establishes the superiority of the gentle sex over the other. This fact is revealed by a naive legend, widely spread in Cambodia. It is repeated where some considerable pious work takes place, building a pond or an artificial mountain. Young men on one side, young ladies on the other are sharing the pious task, and by a mutual challenge try to outdo each other in fervor to see who will finish first. The young ladies can hear the boys challenging each other, promising to rest only during the short moments between the rising of the morning star and the first light of the day. Our Cambodian mischievous ladies hang a lantern at the top of a tree in the direction of that star. Mislead by this trick, the young men rest a big part of the night and are defeated by the young ladies who redouble their efforts.[1]

It is true that this detestable breed of thinker, from which Cambodia is not exempted, pretends that this custom simply comes from the sentiment of obligation that the son-in-law contracts towards those who give him a wife after having given birth to her, fed her and brought her up.

### Births

Cambodian midwives (*iey chhmap*) enjoy a great reputation. In the same way as with the Annamese, a scorching fire is lit up on a stove near the mother to be. A man, an expert (*kru*), encircles the place where she is resting with a cotton thread, so forming a boundary that she must not cross before a few days. This sacred barrier (*sema*) keeps away the bad spirits. When the fire is no longer necessary, the stove is turned upside down and some presents are given to the midwife.

### Funerals

When a Cambodian man is close to dying, his family invites monks to come and recite a prayer called *bang sekaul*. From the beginning of the agony to the certified death of the person, all the laymen and laywomen being present repeat loudly: "Araheang, araheang (the saint, the just)." The dead body is washed

---

[1] We heard this legend for the first time at the pond of *Prea Trepeang* (Sacred Pond) which gave its Cambodian name to our province of *Travenk*. It is a vast two or three hundred meter rectangular excavation, the soil of which was piled up on the sides. It is located at the end of one of the shady alleys which made *Travenk* one of the most pleasant places in French Cochinchina before the terrible hurricane on 24 October 1872.

and wrapped up in a white piece of cotton. A small silver coin or a gold or silver ring is placed in his mouth. He is then put inside a coffin and the monks recite the *bang sekaul* prayer three times on that day and three times the following night. His wife and children dress in white.

In the case of poor people, the cremation takes place almost immediately after the death of a person; if they cannot afford a coffin, they use a straw container instead, called *choeung kak*. Those who are not so poor, generally, burn the body after three days. The rich keep it at home for several months, sometimes several years. They inject it with mercury, and from the coffin a tube goes up to the roof of the house, allowing the gas to escape; this precaution is enough for the indolent Cambodian people. Others bury the body in order to exhume and burn the bones a few years later.

During the cremation, an experienced layman familiar with the old custom is chosen to prepare and conduct the ceremony; he has the title *louki*. He chooses two children within the late person's family. One of them will be the Neak Prai Leech (the one of the whitened and scattered rice), no doubt to teach everyone how little value our body has, all of which disappears, even the whitened and scattered bones. The other child, the Neak Nam Phlau (the guide), wears a long plait made of *sebau* grass (a type of grass which often is used to cover the huts) around his head, The loose end of the plait is attached to the coffin. The Neak Nam Phlau's duty is to guide the late person's soul (*prelung*) straight to the place of bliss, *sokote phup*.

Five monks were invited to recite prayers all the way to the location chosen for the cremation. One of them is carried on a palanquin at the front of the procession, the others go with the coffin holding its four corners. The *louki* positions himself near the porters, in front of the coffin. With one hand he holds the white cotton cloth called the banner, the banner of the soul (*tong prelung*), and with the other he carries a brand new small cooking pot made of clay by means of a white cordon wrapped around the neck of that pot. Moreover, in a shoulder bag he carries the presents given to him by the family: scissors to cut the arec, a lime vase for the betel, and everything that is needed to chew the betel, an operation which he consciously carries out during the ceremony. The cooking pot is supposed to symbolise the fragility of life and the cotton cloth, the vanity of human beings constantly busy putting their fineries on. One must take off all one's ornaments and enter naked into one's grave.

Once everything has been prepared, the coffin is first moved, then pulled outside. Some other monks, in more or less great number, according to whether the dead person is rich or poor, recite the *bang sekaul* prayer in the home and for a last time; they are given the usual presents. The procession starts with a monk at its head, then the two children, *nam phlau* and *prai leech*. Behind them come the *louki* and the four porters, all dressed in white, and finally the family walking behind the coffin. The four porters, called *neak phluk*, who have arrived at the designated location for the cremation, plant four posts into the ground between which they place some wood. The monks recite the *bang sekaul* and the coffin is laid on the pyre after having been carried around it three times. The fire is set by the *louki* at the head of the coffin, by the porters at its four corners, by the family at the bottom, and then by all the relatives, friends and neighbors, some spreading the fire, others lighting some fragrant sticks (*thuk*) which they throw into the coffin, the massive and sculpted cover of which has been taken away in order to be used again. Big logs of wood, placed across the coffin, prevent the dead body from having strong contractions.

It is when the fire is burning fully that people are free to shed tears, to loudly let out their regrets, their groans, their sobs.

Once the pyre has been consumed, the *louki* and the porters, each standing in their place, holding a small jar full of water in their hands, put out the fire. Then they throw their jar onto the other side of the hearth in order to smash it. This is to pass on the message that man, after his death, has no other value than that pot which has been smashed and thrown away.

The hearth is left intact until the next morning, the moment when the sons or grandsons go there taking a coconut, some water in a small jar, and some clay or china vases. They gather the ashes, the coal, the remaining bones so as to form a human body lying on the ground. They cut the coconut in two, collect the water and the two halves of the shell are placed on both sides of the ashes.

The non-consumed bones are then washed with the water from the coconut, mixed with the water from the jar, and then they are placed inside the vases. In the past they were kept inside the home; today this is not done anymore. Most people bury them underneath temples or pagodas, others bury them anywhere.

A Cambodian cemetery with monks, 1866-1875, MAE

## 19 - CELEBRATIONS AND FESTIVALS

Following old customs, for each month of the year the Cambodians have a celebration, the name of which is often borrowed from the old language. The late king, very much attached to traditions, used to scrupulously observe these festivities which have an important place in the customs of the country, and which are always accompanied by prayers recited by the monks plus some offerings to the latter.

1 - In the month of *Chet* (which approximately corresponds to April) there is the celebration of the new year (*Bon Chaul Chhnam*). The day before people build two to three cubit high little sand mounds, (*pun phnom khsach*), five of them, in front of the pagodas or underneath tall trees, under the sacred fig tree (*dem pou*), or on top of mountains. On that first night, after the prayers of the monks, the laymen and women, for fear of de-

Musicians at the royal palace, 1866-1875, MAE

terioration, watch the mounds calling upon *Prea Chet Dey*. In the morning, after another prayer from the monks, followed by pious offerings, the followers go and wash the statues of Buddha in the pagodas. The mounds, encircled by a small bamboo fence with banners and paper umbrellas, are later abandoned to the deeds of nature and animals. For this occasion, a few Cambodians prepare some trestles on which they lay water jars aimed at refreshing the passers by. Others build some shelters and put some sugar or even some perfumes in warm water for people to have a wash. This festivity is observed by the whole kingdom, from the king to the poorest, even if the latter put only one spoonful of rice into the monks' bowl. For some it lasts seven days, for most people three days during which work is suspended. The first day of the festivity is called *Thngay Maha Sangkran Chaul*, the second *Thngay Vahn Bat*, and the third *Thngay Long Sahk*.

2 - In *Pisahk* (May) the agriculture celebration takes place (*Bon Cherat Prea Angkahl*, to lean on the divine plough). Today this royal festivity is obsolete. In the morning of the day fixed by astrologers (*hora*), all the mandarins used to accompany the king to the designated rice field (*prea sre*), which had been fenced off. The *pohuletep*, storeman on the left, yoked the bull on the left, the *pipheak saley*, the bull on the right. Another mandarin led the harness and the king traced three furrows. The store men finished ploughing the field, the harvest of which they carefully husked and which then the king gave to the monks. The inhabitants of the kingdom ploughed their own rice fields only after the end of this ceremony, otherwise they were subject to fines in aid of the store men (*chaufai khleang*).

3 - In *Ches* (June), there is the celebration of the religious ordination (*Bambuos Khnan*). If the king intends to have small mandarins, *khun, moeun, mahalek*, or princesses having turned

A racing canoe used at *Bon Om Touk* water festival, 1866-1874, MAE

twenty, joining a religious order, he orders the preparation, in large quantity, of complete monks' outfits as well as instruments such as bowls, razors, sharpening stones, shoulder bags, boxes for lime. After the monks have recited some prayers in the throne room, an erudite lay person (*acha*) recites special formulas in order to attract blessings onto the *neak*; this is what one calls those who joined a religious order on that day. Then he ties a cotton thread around their wrist (*chang day neahk* or *khvan neahk*). During that night one watches over the *neak* while playing different musical instruments, and in the morning the *neak*, on horse back or on a palanquin, are taken to the pagoda by the king accompanied by his mandarins. An *opechhea* and twenty monks conduct the ordination. With ordinary people, those whose sons are of age to join a religious order gather to perform the same ceremony, but in a more humble way.

4 - In *Asath* (July), the celebration of the beginning of the rainy season takes place (*Bon Chaul Prea Vosa*). Big one meter high torches made of wax are prepared; they are the torches of the expectation of the rainy season (*tien cham prea vosa*). The flame of these torches must be kept constantly burning until the end of the rainy season, except if they are not sufficient and have to be replaced by oil lamps. Everybody prepares some torches; several houses of poor people tend to group themselves in order to offer one or two.

The festival takes place on the day of the full moon. The king, accompanied by his mandarins, goes and offers the monks his torches, to which he adds the usual presents. Also, in a procession, the people take to the monks their oil and torches which they keep either in the temple or in their dwelling. From that day, one or two monks continually watch over the flame. People today still observe this celebration rather regularly.

5 - During the month of *Srap* (August), the festival of flower picking (*Bon Be Phoka*) used to take place, which people partly still observe. The monks are invited to go on a junk to the lakes and the ponds, so numerous in the country, to pick water lilies (*chhuk*) and *prelut* (a kind of small white water lily). There the laymen, as soon as the monks have had their meal, enjoy themselves jousting and boat racing. Everyone goes back home after having picked flowers which will later be given as offerings to Buddha and to monks. This celebration lasts one, two or three days.

6 - In *Phatrabot* (September - October), the big festival of offerings to the ancestors (*Bon Phchum Ben*, in Cambodian, festival of food gathering) takes place. From the first day of the waning moon, everybody, mandarins, men and women vigorously get ready for this festival. Shelters are built for the travellers, the 'sala' are repaired as well as the pagodas. Everyday some take food to the pagoda; others invite the monks to come and have their meal at their house. People give them clothes

as presents. Finally, on the last day of the month a room is prepared inside the house where people put food, cakes, sweets as well as candles and joss sticks, then the whole lot is given as an offering to the ancestors whom one invites, repeating the following invocation three times: "You, our ancestors who departed this life, deign to come and eat what we are offering you and bless your posterity, make them happy".

7 - In *Asoch* (October), there is the festival of the end of the rainy season (*Bon Chenh Prea Vosa*). From the morning on the day of the full moon, regarded by the monks as the last day of the rainy season, the monks are invited to dine at the palace. Boats are prepared for the contests in the evening, which the king attends and which takes place three days in a row. Everywhere, clothes and utensils for monks are offered to thank them for keeping the fire burning during the whole rainy season. The Cambodians call this *he kathen*. Until the full moon, for one month, day and night, to the sound of musical instruments, processions walk the streets of Phnom Penh, taking those offerings to the pagoda of their choice. The princesses, carried on palanquin, go past followed by a bevy of young girls wearing bright colored scarves tinted with those pretty nuances of which only the Cambodians seem to have the secret. The river, the bed of which is still filling up, is crossed by elegant junks transporting a whole indigenous orchestra whose soft melody is charming in the middle of those beautiful and cool nights at that time of year.

Poor people who can only offer the two main pieces of monks' outfit, the coat (*chipo*) and the *langouti* (*sebang*), replace the *he kathen* with the *phapha*. They dress posts with these clothes, and at night, lighting candles and joss sticks, they stealthily plant these posts close to the habitation of the monks, bang loudly on the partitions of the latter and run away as if to avoid being seen by the monks who get up to take these clothes.

8 - In the month of *Kadak* (November) takes place the festival of the floating of small rafts (*Loi Kantong* or *Bandet Prea Tup*, depending on the size of the rafts). This festival is also called the salutation to the moon (*Sampea Prea Khe*). During the three days of festivity, canoe racing takes place in the presence of the king. At night, people bow to the moon and onto the water they throw small bamboo rafts carrying the usual presents, food, candles, arec, joss sticks. The whole lot is offered to *Prea Kong-kea*. On the day of the full moon, food in abundance is offered to the monks. The following night, the laymen go to the pagoda, offer ground green rice (*ambok*) as well as other presents. They worship the moon then get all excited in playing, wrestling, eating mouths full of the ground green rice (*ak ambok*).

9 - In the month of *Mekhaser* (December), people fly kites (*Banghor Khleng*). The late king used to observe this old custom and order his mandarins to make these toys which, due to a constant northeasterly wind blowing at that time of year, and by means of a small instrument attached to it, make an incessant noise, without doubt harmonious to the Khmer ears. On the day of the full moon, the monks were invited to come and have their meal in the throne room, and at night the king and his mandarins launched their kites which they offered to the celestial spirits. The Cambodian people did not abandon this amusement, and the continuous whirring that it makes during the night is quite unpleasant to a European suffering from insomnia.

10 - In the month of *Bos* (January) was the celebration of going into retreats (*Chaul Baveas*). The king had shelters (*roung*) built in the forest, away from the community. Each shelter was surrounded by small huts (*top*) and in each of these huts, a monk retreated for nine days, trying to recite prayers without a break, without sleeping. The shelters were used for meals and for the eminent monks who in groups of four took it in turn to encourage the others. Every morning the king and the mandarins brought them food, water, candles, joss sticks, arec and betel. We are

told that in Laos a similar celebration exists, but in that country with dissolute habits, it is the young girls who bring the presents to the solitary monks.

11 - In *Meahk* (February) used to take place the procession of the *Meahk* (*He Meahk* or *Ba Meahk*). All the mandarins and the governors of provinces went to the capital, together with the *Bakou*, the *Prea Vong* and the *Meahk* king (*sdach*). The latter is a mandarin with 10 *pahn* whose honorific dignity is hereditary in a family of *Prea Vong*; sons succeed their father, the younger brothers their elder brothers, in the same way as for a monarchy.

A bamboo frame was erected and surrounded by sheaves of rice showing the ear outside. It was called the rice mountain (*Phnom Srau*). On the right day, indicated by the astrologists, all the mandarins triumphantly accompanied the *Sdach Meahk*. They were equipped in accordance with their functions; some were on horse back, others on elephant back, others in carts. The *Sdach Meahk* himself rode an elephant or was carried on the royal palanquin. Some slave-soldiers (*pol*), weapon bearers, in this triumphal procession represented the neighboring populations of Annam, Siam, Laos, etc..., whose uniforms they wore. The king, having the grand mandarins next to him, sat under his pavilion to watch the procession. On another platform, the women of the court used to sit. The *Meahk* king dismounted when he reached the level of the real king and bowed at the feet of the latter who granted him the dignity of king for three days, and therefore all the income taxes or revenues which came in during this lapse of time. It is true that for a long time now, this latter practice has become obsolete.

After the third day's procession, the *Sdach Meahk* ordered the mandarins on elephants' back to upset and trample on the rice mountain, from all sides at the same time. Ordinary men took away some of the rice; it was supposed to bring them a prosperous harvest. The rice which remained attached to the stalk was again trampled on and brought to the king who boiled it and gave to the monks.

Today this ceremony has been replaced by an exhibition (*Teang To*, this is a Chinese name, but the Cambodian expression is *Kruong Bauchea Tevada*) provided by the governors of the provinces and the mandarins of the interior with eight *pahn* and more, who for some, exhibit within the palace, for others, outside the palace, whatever remarkable items they have: wood, flowers, statues, horns, carpets, etc..., etc..., even our articles from Paris and our hardware. Some sheds are erected for various theatres, and, depending on the number of *sahk*, the governors provide food for the dancers and even money if the latter are very demanding.

On the last day of this celebration, the king has his head shaved, the Siamese way. The *Bakou* then pour water, contained in shells, on his head. Then the king bows in front of the monks, who recite blessing and prosperity prayers, and gives them his presents when they have had their meal. It is the personal festivity of the current king who was born during that month. The Cambodians name it the festival of blessing, wishes of prosperity for the holy existence (*Bon Chamroeun Prea Chun*).

12 - Finally, in *Phalkun* (March), used to take place the festival of chasing away bad spirits (*Bandenh Khmoch*, also called *Banchahn Tras*, trample on the bad spirits). Debris of statues, stones regarded as the stay of those reprobates, were collected and taken to the capital where elephants had been gathered in as big a number as possible. Behind the palace, some sheds were built facing the eight points of the horizon. And on the day of the full moon, inside each shed four monks used to come and pray, altogether thirty-two, selected among those who had a loud voice and who knew the prayer *Pheaneiiahk*. Other monks recited the usual prayers in the throne room. In the evening, armed men discharged their guns and the elephants uttered furious discharges in order to chase away the bad spirits. This used to take

place three days in a row.

Today this festival, called *Krut Sangkran* or *Chun Chhnam Tras Tou*, takes place only for things relating to the monks.

A Cambodian royal musician, 1866-1875, MAE

An actress at the royal palace of the King of Cambodia, 1866-1875, MAE

# APPENDIX

## MEASURES - MONEYS - WEIGHTS

### Measures Of Length

The cubit (*hat*) = about 0,40. The brass (*phieem*) = 5 hat = about 2 m. For fabrics, the *thbaung* = 19 hat, that is 4 metres.

For distances: the *sen* = 20 phieem or 40 metres; 100 *sen* (*moroi sen*) or simply *moroi,* equivalent to 4 kilometres. It is a very well known measure in Cambodia. The *me-iouch* = 400 sen = 16 kilometres, is seldom used.

The submultiples of the *hat* are : the chamam (length covered by the spread thumb and little finger of a hand) = 1/2 hat = 20 centimetres; the *chamam* is subdivided into 12 *thnahp* (breadth of a finger); the *thnahp* into 12 *krahp srau* (rice grain); the krahp srau into 12 *khluon chay* (a louse); the khluon chay into 12 *pong chay* (a nit); the *pong chay* in 8 *anu* (a grain of sand); the *anu* in 8 *abhamanu* (a speck of dust).

### Measures Of Capacity

These measures for rice are: the *thang*, equivalent to the Annamese *gia*, the multiples of which are: the load (*modek*) = 20 *thang*; the cartload (*mo rote*) = 80 *thang*.

The *thang* is subdivided into 2 *tau* or *kanchseu* (basket); the *tau* into 2 *kan teang* ; the *kan teang* into 2 *kombang* (content of two open hands); the *kombang* into 2 *luk day* (content of one open hand); the *luk day* into 2 *kedap* (a closed hand); the *kedap* in 8 *cheyp* (one pinch).

### Moneys (Kas, Prak)

The moneys used in Cambodia are:

1 - the silver bar (*nen*) which can currently be exchanged for 15 piastres or 100 'ligatures' of sapeques;

2 - The Mexican piastre (*rihl bareang*), which is spreading more and more;

3 - As small cash, the 'ligature' of sapeque (*trenot kas*) which in the same way as the Annamese, they divide in 10 *tien* (*tinh*).

It is important to know a few expressions relating to the money of an account often used, particularly in the jargon of law:

1 - The *anching* = 80 *bat*, that is 320 'ligatures.'

2 - The *damleng* = 4 *bat* or 16 'ligatures.'

3 - The bat or *riklluong* = 4 'ligatures.'

4 - The sleng thom = 1 'ligature.'

5 - The sleng tau*c*h or *prak pram hu*n = 1/2 'ligature.'

6 - The hun = 1/10 'ligature' or 1 *tien*.

The moneys 1, 2 and 6 are fictitious; they have never been struck.

[A 'ligature' is 600 Annamite sapeques, a zinc disc pierced in the center, strung together to form one 'ligature,' worth one franc.]

## Weights

The weight measures used in Cambodia are:

1 - The pikul, *hap* = about 60 kilograms.

2 - The *chong* = 1/2 *pikul* = about 30 kilograms.

3 - The *neel* = 1/60 *chong* = 600 grams.

4 - The damleng = 1/10 *neel* = 37.5 grams.

5 - The *chi* = 1/10 *damleng* = 3.75 grams.

6 - The *hun* = 1/10 *chi* = 0.375 gram.

7 - The *li* = 1/10 *hun* = 0.0375 gram.

8 - The *ho* = 1/10 *li* = 0.00375 gram.

9 - The *hut* = 1/10 *ho* = 0.000375 gram.

## CYCLE - ERA - SEASONS

### Cycle

The Cambodians have a duodenary cycle which, when repeated five times, forms the big cycle of sixty years. The years are named as follows:

*Chhnam Chhlau*, Year Of The Ox.
"       *Khal*, Year Of The Tiger.
"       *Thar*, Year Of The Hare.
"       *Roung*, Year Of The Dragon.
"       *Mesanh*, Year Of The Snake.
"       *Momi*, Year Of The Horse.
"       *Mome*, Year Of The Goat.
"       *Vok*, Year Of The Monkey.
"       *Roka*, Year Of The Rooster.
"       Cha, Year Of The Dog.
"       *Kor*, Year Of The Pig.
"       Chut, Year Of The Rat.

The big cycle of 60 years is divided in six decades or *chuor* (rows), in everyone of which the years are numbered from the first to the tenth by the number followed by the ending sahk.

The year 1874, from the Christian era, corresponds to the Cambodian year *Cha Chhasahk*, the year *cha*, 6th of the decade, the 1236th of the era *Cholosahkreach*, and the 2417th of the era *Putsah Reach*.

### Era (Sahkreach)

The Cambodians have three eras, their names are stated below, as well as their years corresponding to the year 1874 of the Christian era.

1 - The era of the Buddha, *Put Sahkreach*, year 2417.

2 - The great era, *Maha Sahkreach*, year 1796.

3 - The small era, *Cholosahkreach*, year 1236. That year is usually used in official acts, in transactions, etc.,

### Seasons (Redaus)

The Cambodians have three seasons:

1 - The rainy season, *Redau Phlieng*.

2 - The cold season, *Redau* Rongear.

3 - The dry or hot season, *Redau Preang*.

### CAMBODIAN ART

Regarding the Cambodian Art, we can only refer to the excellent work titled: *L'Art Khmer, The Khmer Art, an historical study of the monuments of the old Cambodia, with a general view on the Khmer architecture plus a complete list of the explored monuments, followed by a reasoned brochure of the Khmer Museum in Compiegne (France), made by Count de Croizier enriched with reproductions of carvings and a map.*[1]

We here show two specimens of images extracted from the above mentioned book.

[On the next page are the only three specimens in that book.]

---

1 Ernest Leroux, publisher, rue Bonaparte, 28. - 1 vol. in 8.

Ornamentation fragment of a pilaster at Melea

Phnom with four faces

Fragment of a sandstone pediment decorated with nine Lakhon (dancers), in high relief, wearing the *sampot* (langoutis) and coiffed with the *mokhoit* (antique tiara)

# NOTES/QUOTES

"To assist his administration, the governor has subordinates whom he appoints himself, or as the Cambodian expression has it, whom he feeds (*chanhchem*). The number of these civil servants, named by the generic title *Kromokar*, therefore, depends on the whim of the governor or on the interest that Cambodians may have in buying a title."

"We will not talk about the Cambodian law in this note. Let us only say that in the Khmer language, sentencing means selling (*lok*); and in actual fact, all cases end up in a sale, with the freeing of the convicted person as a forfeit if he does not redeem himself by paying the amount of the sentencing."

"The government of Cambodia is an absolute monarchy. The king is the only Master, the one and only owner of the kingdom. He appoints and removes the great mandarins and the governors of the provinces as he pleases. He sets the taxes, he makes the laws; he is the supreme magistrate. Everything goes back to him and follows from him."

www.ingramcontent.com/pod-product-compliance
Lightning Source LLC
Chambersburg PA
CBHW081402080526
44588CB00016B/2567